CRAVE DALLAS

The Urban Girl's Manifesto

Melody Biringer

CRAVE Dallas: The Urban Girl's Manifesto

A publication of The CRAVE Company
1805 12th Ave W #A
Seattle WA 98119
206.282.0173

thecravecompany.com/dallas
twitter.com/cravedallas
facebook.com/cravedallas

While every effort was made to ensure the accuracy of the information, details are subject to change, so please call ahead. Neither The CRAVE Company nor CRAVE Dallas shall be responsible for any consequences arising from this publication or the use of it.

All editorial content in this publication is the sole opinion of CRAVE Dallas and our contributing writers. No fees or services were rendered in exchange for inclusion in this publication.

Printed in the United States of America

ISBN 978-0-9847143-7-7
Second Edition
November 2012
$19.95 USD

The Urban Girl's Manifesto

We CRAVE Community.

We believe in acknowledging, celebrating and passionately supporting local businesses. CRAVE is a celebration of women entrepreneurs that showcases creative, interesting and gutsy proprietors. By introducing you to the savvy businesswomen in this guide, we hope that we will help inspire your own inner entrepreneur.

We CRAVE Adventure.

We encourage you to break your routine, to venture away from your regular haunts, to visit new businesses, to explore all the funky finds and surprising spots that the Dallas metropolitan area has to offer. Whether it's to hunt for a birthday gift, indulge in a spa treatment or connect with like-minded people, let *CRAVE Dallas* be your guide for a one-of-a-kind hometown adventure.

We CRAVE Quality.

CRAVE is all about quality products and thoughtful service. We know that a satisfying shopping trip requires more than a simple exchange of money for goods, and that a rejuvenating spa date entails more than a quick clip of the cuticles and a swipe of polish. We know you want to come away feeling uplifted, beautiful, excited, relaxed, relieved and, above all, knowing you got the most bang for your buck. We have scoured the city to find the hidden gems, new hot spots and old standbys, all with one thing in common: they're the best of the best!

A Guide to Our Guide

CRAVE Dallas is more than a guidebook. It's a savvy, lifestyle book devoted entirely to local businesses owned by women. *CRAVE Dallas* will direct you to some of the best local spots—top boutiques, spas, cafés, stylists, fitness studios and more. And we'll introduce you to the inspired, dedicated women behind these exceptional enterprises, for whom creativity, quality, innovation and customer service are paramount.

Not only is *CRAVE Dallas* an intelligent guide for those wanting to know what's happening throughout town, but it's also a directory for those who value the contributions that spirited businesswomen make to our region.

2shea Boutique and TrueBeautyRx

Lakewood, Dallas

Fresh. Unique. Stylish.

2shea Boutique is the latest venture of Dallas entrepreneur Shea Boothe-Wood. This fabulous boutique features on-trend yet one-of-a-kind fashions and gives personal attention to style. 2shea Boutique incorporates Shea's background in fashion design with her experience in the skincare industry. Modern white decor with accents of hot pink and orange is the perfect backdrop for her oil paintings, 2shea clothing collection and amazing jewelry. Fashion, beauty, art... what more could a girl ask for?

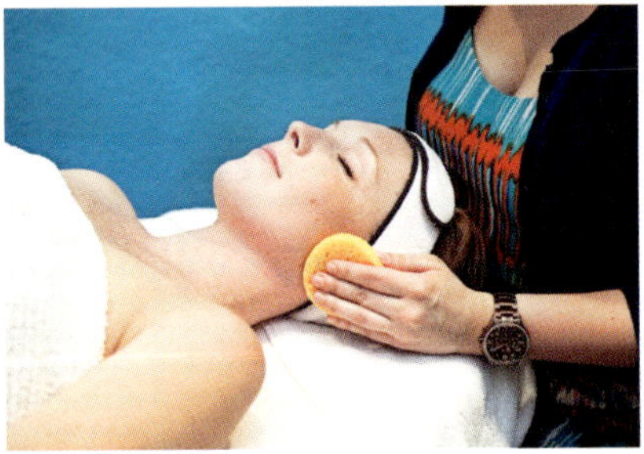

Photos by Elle Parks Photography

Specialties: Fashion, Beauty, Art
2shea Boutique: 6342 La Vista Drive, Ste B, Dallas, 214.272.3652
2sheaboutique.com, facebook.com/2SheaBoutique
Twitter: @2SheaBoutique
TrueBeautyRx: 6224 La Vista Drive, Dallas, 214.434.1664
truebeautyrx.com, Twitter: @TrueBeautyRx

Shea Boothe-Wood

Q&A

What tip would you give women who are starting a business?
Believe in your passion, trust yourself and ask a lot of questions. Listen and surround yourself with those you can learn from and always remember to give back!

Who is your role model or mentor?
My father. An entrepreneur himself, he taught me firsthand the importance of integrity, the foundation of business: the lessons he learned from failing and the joy of success. He also encouraged me to never give up.

What motivates you on a daily basis?
The people I love in my life motivate me. Knowing that today is such a gift and to cherish every moment. Remembering that life is short and that I have a lot I want to accomplish is what motivates me the most.

Photos by Misti Davis of Pink Fly Photography, except lower right photo by Jay Davis of Jay Davis Photography

A Well Dressed Home

Dallas, Texas

Sophisticated. Chic. Fresh.

A Well Dressed Home is a testimony to sophisticated, stylish yet affordable design. While keeping a practical budget in mind, Emily Hewett is able to turn houses into stylish homes. A Well Dressed Home can help you create beautiful spaces for less as they offer a combination of design services that can be tailored to meet your needs.

Emily Hewett,
Allied ASID

Q&A

What are your most popular products or services?

The Online Design Board is our most popular service as it provides stylish, affordable design to clients outside of the Dallas/Ft. Worth area.

What do you like best about owning a business?

Everything! But what I love most is being responsible for driving the company in a direction in which I feel it will thrive.

What place inspires you?

I feel most inspired while flipping through the pages of shelter magazines and scrolling through design blogs, especially when I come across something daring and unexpected.

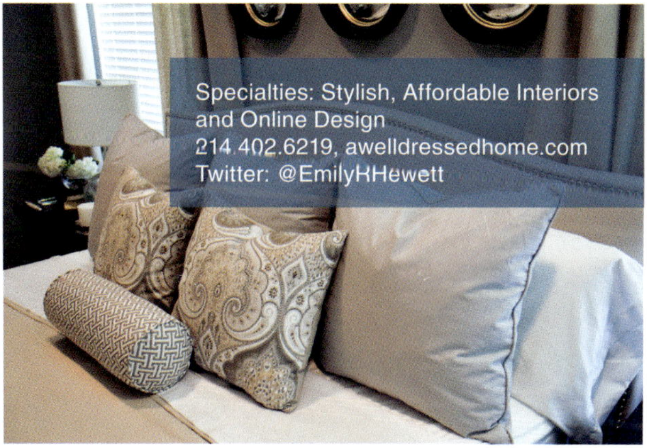

Specialties: Stylish, Affordable Interiors and Online Design
214.402.6219, awelldressedhome.com
Twitter: @EmilyRHewett

Q&A

What are your most popular products or services?
Hair and makeup services for special events, keratin straightening treatments and Great Lengths hair extensions.

What is your motto or theme song?
Don't be afraid to reinvent yourself when necessary.

What place inspires you?
I'm inspired most when I'm out on the water sailing. That's where I'm at peace and can reflect and think about all aspects of my life.

What do you like best about owning a business?
Being my own boss and seeing my creative ideas come to life.

Ashley Russell & Company Salon

Oak Lawn, Dallas

Stylish. Fabulous. Fun.

Ashley Russell & Company Salon is a full-service salon specializing in the latest styles and trends for women and men. Clients are provided with outstanding customer service in a homey setting located in a unique historic house.

Photos by Kelly Rucker Photography, except portrait by Gittings

Asian Mint

Asian Fusion Cafe and Dessert Bar

Preston Hollow, Highland Park and North Dallas

Soul-satisfying. Addictive. Unique.
Asian Mint offers only fresh ingredients in their Asian-inspired dishes in a comfy, cool atmosphere coupled with hospitable service. As a "Top 10 Best New Restaurants" recipient awarded by the Dallas Morning News, they invite you to come and satisfy your soul with the best pad Thai in town, signature martinis and Asian-fused desserts like their green tea cake and jasmine crème brûlée.

Specialties: Asian Fusion Cuisine, Desserts, Full Bar
asianmint.com, Twitter: @TheMintDallas
facebook.com/AsianMintDallas
Asian Mint—Asian Fusion Cafe and Dessert Bar:
11617 N Central Expwy, Ste 135, Dallas, 214.363.6655
The Mint—Asian Fusion Cafe:
4246 Oak Lawn Ave, Dallas, 214.219.6468

Photos by Rebecca Fondren, except portrait by Catie Ronquillo

Q&A

What are your most popular products or services?
Pad Thai in five different versions, sakejito, green tea cake, mango martinis, full bar, dollar sushi nights, steamed sea bass, vegetarian-friendly, gluten-free menu.

What tip would you give women who are starting a business?
Have a business plan with financials. Revisit your executive summary when you are lost or get off track. Do things with the best intentions and work ethic. Be honest!

What do you like best about owning a business?
Helping others and seeing your dreams come true. Positively touching other people's souls and making a difference in the world, one dish at a time. Spreading the love.

Faryn Masso Clark and Nanci Masso

Q&A

What are your most popular products or services?
Lose-it Advantage, The Magic Cookie and Optinol are used for weight loss and maintaining health. Even more convenient and effective is to use them together in the Lose-it Challenge.

What tip would you give women who are starting a business?
Have a goal in mind. If you don't, you just work, work, work with no vision of where you are going and what you want at the end of the day.

How do you relax?
We enjoy playing tennis together and traveling all over the world.

Biosanes Nutrition and Health

Dallas, Texas

Healthy. Great-tasting. All-natural.

Biosanes Nutrition and Health was founded by a mother-daughter team that has a passion for health, nutrition and weight loss. Biosanes has great-tasting products that assist in providing excellent nutrition and easy ways to lose weight. The products are all-natural and have organic ingredients. Biosanes makes it easy to be healthy with products that are convenient for your busy life.

Photos by Leslie Katz, except portrait by Claire McCormack

Bookkeeper Girl

Denton, Texas

Affordable. Trustworthy. Personable.

Bookkeeper Girl is America's bookkeeper providing online, trustworthy bookkeeping services. Initially launched in Denton, Texas, they quickly grew into remote offices in Dallas and then Austin, and now provide services for national customers alike. Bookkeeper Girl has been nationally recognized by Tory Johnson in her book *Spark & Hustle*, and is the ultimate solution for small-business owners who need bookkeeping and payroll services.

Photos by Elle Parks Photography

Specialties: Bookkeeping, Payroll Services
By appointment: 100 W Oak, Ste G-111, Denton, 866.960.9787
bookkeepergirl.com, facebook.com/bookkeepergirl
Twitter: @bookkeepergirl, linkedin.com/in/bookkeepergirl

Kim Pollard

Q&A

Who is your role model or mentor?
Tory Johnson knows how to take adversity and turn it into success. Steve Jobs was such an innovator, and he inspires me to look for new ways to implement technology.

What is your motto or theme song?
"Gotta have faith!" I believe that my faith—in my company, employees, customers, family and God—leads to my success. I don't have time to doubt!

What do you like best about owning a business?
At the end of the day, I like knowing that we've helped make other people's lives better, either through inspiration, volunteerism or a service they need that helps them grow.

Photo by Elle Parks Photography

"When starting a business, dream big and have faith. Have a vision and do not minimize your dreams. Surround yourself with cheerleaders; then have faith and believe that you will make it. And never, ever quit."

—Kim Pollard of Bookkeeper Girl

Specialty: Promotional Marketing
972.567.1064, boundlesscollection.com
facebook.com/BoundlessCollection
linkedin.com/in/AmberGeorge

Amber George

Q&A

What are your most popular products or services?
We provide a wide array of marketing services. We are best known for providing clients with smart promotional merchandise options that effectively represent their brand and marketing initiatives.

What tip would you give women who are starting a business?
Invest in *people*! I have an amazing, passionate and creative team that truly cares about our customers. Our staff is my daily inspiration and the reason we have loyal clients.

What do you CRAVE?
Being “in the moment” with good friends and family. Recognizing how wonderful those moments are.

Boundless Collection

Creative. Inspiring. Rewarding

Boundless Collection is a full-service promotional marketing agency providing branded promotional merchandise and corporate gifts that are creative, impressive and impactful. With over twelve years of experience, Amber George and her team are true industry experts... dedicated and passionate about finding exciting, creative and inspiring products. Simply put, their mission is to make marketing through corporate gifts and employee incentives memorable and effective.

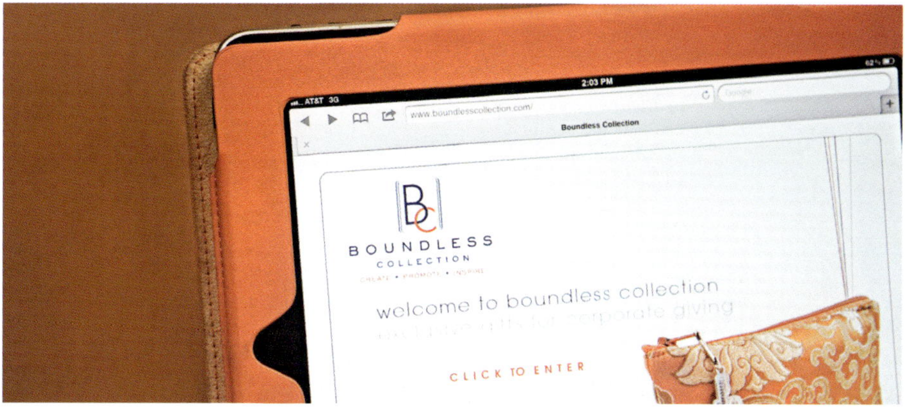

Photos by Elle Parks Photography

Specialties: Frozen Yogurt, Catering, Push Pops, Shaved Ice
603 S Main St, Ste 302, Grapevine
817.410.4650, cassiesfrozenyogurt.com
facebook.com/CassiesFrozenYogurt

Portrait and lower left photo by Catie Ronquillo

Cassie's Frozen Yogurt

Grapevine, Texas

Colorful. Creative. Bold.

Cassie's Frozen Yogurt is based in Grapevine but has concession locations at Allen Events Center, Dallas Market Center and the State Fair. Cassie's also offers a variety of unique and delicious catering options ranging from frozen yogurt bars to gourmet push pops. Cassie's is the only company in Texas that serves a variety of Jelly Belly–licensed frozen treats!

Cassie Uptmore

Q&A

Who is your role model or mentor?
My mother. She is the most inspirational, generous, loving, charismatic, engaging, driven, patient and successful woman. I consider it a privilege and an honor to have her in my life!

What tip would you give women who are starting a business?
Have patience and be strong. Remember that this is a marathon, not a sprint. Don't let the setbacks hold you back. Tomorrow is a new day!

What is your motto or theme song?
Both my mottoes come straight from my dad. I hated both of them growing up, but now I say them almost every day: "Life's a long time" and "Buck up, Buckaroo."

Photo by Catie Ronquillo

"I love waking up daily knowing that everything I do (good and bad) will affect my business. Sometimes I like to think I'm in my own version of The Apprentice*."*

—Cassie Uptmore of Cassie's Frozen Yogurt

Catie Ronquillo Photography

Dallas, Texas

Bright. Inspired. Authentic.

Catie Ronquillo Photography is a boutique photography studio specializing in multicultural weddings for couples who want to honor their heritage, celebrate their union and begin building a legacy together that is uniquely their own. Catie believes in the importance of honoring the past and growing together in marriage. She is a lifestyle and wedding photographer, based in Dallas and available for commissions worldwide.

Specialty: Wedding Photography
214.302.7911
catieronquillo.com, Twitter: @CatieRonquillo
facebook.com/catieronquillophoto

Photos by Catie Ronquillo, except portrait by Maggie McDonald Photography

Q&A

What tip would you give women who are starting a business?
Never give up. There will always be days when you want to throw in the towel, but it's those days when you are on the brink of a breakthrough.

What is your biggest fear?
Playing it safe. Being too scared of taking a risk.

What place inspires you?
I'll always have a special place in my heart for Lyon, France. I studied abroad there, experienced the culture and made lifelong friendships.

How do you relax?
Watching movies at home on the couch with my husband.

Photos by Katie Cassidy Photography

Chalkboard China & Agency Entourage

Dallas, Texas

Creative. Elegant. Proven.

Chalkboard China is a collection of chalk-friendly vases, wine glasses, serving pieces, carafes and more that you can decorate and re-decorate for every occasion. Featured in 750+ retailers nationwide. As seen on *Good Morning America*, *The View*, and *The Today Show*, Agency Entourage is the award-winning digital marketing agency behind Chalkboard China and is ready to take your product/brand where you dream it can go.

Candace Jean Neff Randolph

Q&A

What do you like best about owning a business?
I love that I have worked in every aspect of my businesses. When you need to spend time in your areas of weakness, it builds you and your character.

What is your motto or theme song?
"I want to leave a legacy. How will they remember me? Did I choose to love? Did I point to You enough?...And leave that kind of legacy." —Nichole Nordeman

What place inspires you?
Seaside, I love that it was a vision that was executed amazingly. I love places full of good design and that carry out their theme to a tee!

Specialties: Communication, Branding

Chalkboard China: 866.774.0109 x704, chalkboardchina.com
facebook.com/ChalkboardChina, Twitter: @chalkboardchina

Agency Entourage: 214.414.3036, agencyentourage.com
facebook.com/agencyentourage, Twitter: @agencyentourage

linkedin.com/in/candaceneffrandolph

Q&A

What tip would you give women who are starting a business?
Always be willing to network with people you meet as they are usually offering great advice; however, stay true to you and your concept. This is what makes you unique.

What place inspires you?
Texas Hill Country. I love to go down to Hill Country and shop the small town boutiques. They are so comfortable, relaxed and fun. Full of history and charm!

How do you relax?
A casual dinner with family, friends and a great glass of wine.

What motivates you on a daily basis?
The pure joy of "playing" in all the new arrivals and visiting with new friends each day.

Chateau Rustic

Frisco, Texas

Unique. Fun. Chic.
Looking to inject some "Hill Country chic" into your North Texas style? Look to Chateau Rustic, the newest addition to Frisco's Main Street, providing a "stop, shop and stay" environment. The concept emulates a relaxed Hill Country setting. A place for girlfriends to gather, share a story and a glass of wine. Fabulous finds for clothing, jewelry, handbags, home decor and very unique furniture pieces.

Photos by Katie Cassidy Photography

Photo by Katie Cassidy Photography

"What I like best about owning a business is bringing in personal style, memories and favorite finds from my favorite travels."

—Allison Schurr of Chateau Rustic

Melissa Wilburn

Q&A

What are your most popular products or services?
Our "Some Like It Hot" grilled Pimiento Cheese Sandwich. It's the best thing to happen to the sandwich since, well, sliced bread. Featured recently in *Southern Living*.

What tip would you give women who are starting a business?
Balance work with wellness. You can run down, run out and run crazy quickly, and you will if you don't guard your health—body, mind and spirit.

What motivates you on a daily basis?
The people who are going to come spend a part of their day with us. Knowing our customers are coming to celebrate a family milestone or linger over a cup of tea.

Chocolate Angel Cafe and Tearoom

Plano, Texas

Tasty. Quaint. Elegant.
If you long for the nostalgic foods of a bygone era, Chocolate Angel Cafe and Tearoom is your cup of tea. Made fresh daily from scratch, their menu includes tasty salads, sandwiches, soups and desserts that remind you of the "good old days." Whether you order the Special of the Day or come for afternoon tea, owner Melissa Wilburn's desire is that you relish the experience of dining with Chocolate Angel.

Photos by Vernie Sandbekkhaug and Claire McCormack

Coco Fleur Events

Dallas, Texas

Stylish. Southern. Creative.
Coco Fleur is a floral event company that takes great pride in designing floral and decor to reflect their clients' style. Coco Fleur strives to hand-pick quality flowers and carefully selects beautiful decor to ensure your event is unique to your individual style and taste.

Specialty: Floral Event Design
cocofleureventdesign.com

Photos by Katie Cassidy Photography

Q&A

What are your most popular products or services?
Beautiful antiques, settees, crystal and silver fixtures such as candelabras, chandeliers and vases.

What tip would you give women who are starting a business?
Never be afraid. Never underestimate yourself. If you believe in and love what you do, others will too. Make friends and talk to others who are in your field.

What motivates you on a daily basis?
Nature inspires me and reminds me of why I do what I do.

How do you relax?
Crazy but true... when I feel stressed I can go out into the studio and arrange flowers!

Photo by Katie Cassidy Photography

"What I like best about owning a business is getting to know my clients. Working so close with them on such a special occasion makes them feel like a part of my family."

—Lisa Ham of Coco Fleur Events

Specialty: Computer Tutoring for Senior Citizens
214.293.2094, ComputerTutor4Seniors.com
facebook.com/conversationcounts, Twitter: @ConvoCounts
linkedin.com/in/BeccaNiederkrom

Becca Niederkrom

Q&A

What are your most popular products or services?
Private tutoring, LinkedIn webinars for my Boomers in Business, and The Computer Tutor Tech Mobile for Retirement Homes with emphasis on our super cool computers and accessories for those who crave simplicity in computing.

What do you like best about owning a business?
Living my life's purpose to be a joyful connector of all people. And the freedom to play out my vision as big as I want while designing an amazing life.

What do you CRAVE?
Love, success, meaningful relationships with my clients, family and friends. I crave becoming a better me with each new moment, each new day.

ComputerTutor4Seniors.com

Dallas, Texas

Simple. Helpful. Caring.

ComputerTutor4Seniors.com works with all baby boomers, senior citizens and retirement home residents who struggle with using the computer and are in need of simplicity and accessibility in their personal and professional lives. ComputerTutor4Seniors.com is the "Technology Superstore for Boomers and Beyond," equipping their awesome clients with the tech gadgets to connect them online with simplicity and slow-and-steady instruction to allow them to truly enjoy the computer.

Photos by Natalie Pitts

Jill Allison Bryan

Q&A

What are your most popular products or services?
One-on-one coaching via phone (I work with clients all over the world), group classes, workshops, teleclasses, retreats and presentations.

What do you like best about owning a business?
The inspiring women I get to meet and work with every day. It's incredibly satisfying to watch them blossom and shine as they create the lives they desire for themselves.

What is your motto or theme song?
"Don't ask what the world needs. Ask what makes you come alive, and go do it. Because what the world needs is people who have come alive." —Howard Thurman

Creative Oasis Coaching

Dallas, Texas

Energizing. Encouraging. Empowering.
If you've ever wished for more time to enjoy creative fulfillment in your busy life, Jill Allison Bryan can help make your wish come true. A certified Master Kaizen-Muse® Creativity Coach, Jill guides and supports you to move past procrastination, perfectionism, overwhelm and other blocks to gently and joyfully create the time and space for creativity and a happier, more satisfying life.

Photos by Elle Parks Photography

Q&A

What are your most popular products or services?
Saving our clients money is a winner! They also find value in how we focus on source reduction and methods of simplifying recycling for their company.

What tip would you give women who are starting a business?
Make choices for your business based on your beliefs, values and what will do the most good. Put people and planet before profits, and be confident in that decision.

What is your biggest fear?
I fear losing my sense of humor in a world that often makes little sense.

What is your motto or theme song?
Kindness regardless.

Creative Waste Solutions

Dallas, Texas

Resourceful. Responsible. Progressive.
Creative Waste Solutions focuses on reducing expenses and increasing recycling through smarter waste management. Their clients are varied and share the common benefit of enjoying real, quantifiable cost savings found in an area that does not affect employee service or customer satisfaction. Creative Waste Solutions will add money to your budget while strengthening your commitment to the environment through waste reduction, diversion and recycling.

Photos by Natalie Pitts, except lower right photo

Cuptastic!

Dallas, Texas

Decadent. Flavorful. Addictive.
Cuptastic! was born out of the passion shared by two sisters, who enjoy baking and love to bring smiles to everyone as they experience their tasty treats. Cuptastic! provides a wide variety of made-from-scratch cupcakes baked with the freshest ingredients and delivered right to your doorstep. Each order is made to give customers the yummiest cupcake experience.

Photos by Natalie Pitts, except lower left photo by Kelly Rucker

Q&A

What tip would you give women who are starting a business?

Follow your passion and develop a plan. Don't get discouraged just because things aren't moving as quickly as you had hoped. Remember good things come to those who wait!

What do you like best about owning a business?

The best thing about it is having creative freedom. The sky is the limit! Our business can go whereever our dreams can take us.

What place inspires you?

Our great-grandmother's kitchen. It's where we grew up! We learned to cook at an early age, hovering around our grandma, watching her cook. Most of our secrets come from Grandma.

Custom Laser Engravers, LLC

Design District, Dallas

Unique. Creative. Clever.
Custom Laser Engravers collaborates with clients to transform ideas onto various materials of the clients' choosing. They can engrave on metals, glass, acrylics, wood and many other unique substrates. They have combined their Fort Worth and Dallas locations to offer a wide array of services as well as gift offerings in the convenient Dallas Design District.

Specialties: Custom Laser and Rotary Engraving and Custom Gifts
1325 Levee St, Dallas, 214.310.8310
customlaserengravers.com
facebook.com/CustomLaserEngravers
linkedin.com/in/customlaserengravers

Photos by Matt & Julie Weddings

Q&A

What tip would you give women who are starting a business?
Know your market and streamline your focus in a way that speaks to your strengths. Be realistic with yourself and honest with the customer about what is truly doable.

Who is your role model or mentor?
My mom. She is an extremely smart businesswoman and has great design taste, which translates well to our engraving projects. She gives me a different perspective.

What motivates you on a daily basis?
Unique project challenges. I look forward to getting those projects dreamed up by our clients and bringing them to life.

Tammy Owens

Q&A

What are your most popular products or services?
The Nutcracker and the Nativity™ because it weaves a holiday classic with the true meaning of Christmas while giving students the chance to be a part of something truly significant.

What do you like best about owning a business?
Creating a one-of-a-kind dance studio that combines my passion for dance and love for God with the joy of working with children.

What place inspires you?
Our beautiful studio. It is a positive, noncompetitive and fun environment where I get to care for children, serve families and encourage the special women who work for me.

Dancing Angels Studio

Dallas, Texas

Unique. Nurturing. Inspiring.
More than tiptoes, twirls and tutus, Dancing Angels Studio is a unique program that nurtures the hearts and spirits of girls. This program, which was born through a love of children, dance and Jesus, goes beyond the traditional studio to inspire its students to dance for the glory of God. From ballet to hip-hop and everything in between, they offer classes, camps, parties and more!

Photos by Mo Sadjapour, except portrait by Katie Cassidy Photography

Deanie Michelle Events

Dallas, Texas

Creative. Fun. Passionate.

Deanie Michelle Events is a full-service wedding and event consulting firm that focuses on a smaller number of clientele to provide service, detail and attention, which makes them feel more like a good friend rather than just another event professional. Each event is beautifully designed, thoughtfully planned and flawlessly executed. They will ease your stress and allow you to be a guest at your own event!

Specialties: Weddings and Nonprofit/Charity Events
214.810.4024, deanie-michelle-events.com
facebook.com/DallasWeddingPlanner.DeanieMichelleEvents
Twitter: @DMEevents

Photos by EE photography, Greg Blomberg, Jimages and Brittany Nicole

Deanie Yuska

Q&A

What are your most popular products or services?
Our full planning package, which enables clients to benefit from our expertise during each stage of the planning process. It is more than just a service, it is an experience.

What tip would you give women who are starting a business?
Follow your passion, hold yourself to a standard of grace rather than perfection, and most importantly, have fun!

How do you relax?
Working out relaxes me. I love running, walking and yoga. Working out keeps me focused day to day. But there's nothing like a spa day to really relax and recharge.

Q&A

What do you like best about owning a business?
I love fashion and being able to contribute to the fashion world. This venture has allowed me to be a part of the community and support animal rescues.

What place inspires you?
Bookstores, flea markets, museums, shopping and hi-lo culture.

What motivates you on a daily basis?
Meeting new customers and making long-lasting relationships and friends.

What do you CRAVE?
Love, life and laughter... and chocolate every now and then.

Ditto Boutique

Lakewood, Dallas

Eclectic. Creative. Fun.

Ditto Boutique features fabulous fashion from high-end European and American designers to amazing hand-picked vintage selections. Artfully arranged in a funky eclectic boutique with a distinct neighborhood atmosphere, Ditto Boutique has become a place where fashionistas shop, and the friendly staff is always welcoming and helpful. Always something fab and fun to see at Ditto Boutique... new and new to you!

Specialties: Consignment, Designer, Vintage, Styling
Hillside Village, 6465 E Mockingbird Lane #362, Dallas
214.370.4444, dittoboutique.weebly.com
facebook.com/dittoboutique, Twitter: @Ditto_Boutique

Photos by Matt & Julie Weddings

Q&A

What tip would you give women who are starting a business?
Believe in what you are selling.

What is your motto or theme song?
Go big or go home.

What place inspires you?
Aspen. Mountain activities and the energy I get from them opens the mind.

Who is your role model or mentor?
My role model is my own vision of my future. See it, believe it, make it happen.

What do you like best about owning a business?
Helping people believe in themselves and empowering them to do the same.

Dive Coastal Cuisine

University Park, Dallas

Fresh. Organic. Real.

Dive is a casual, convenient and deliciously healthy option for the on-the-go foodie at an affordable price. With light and flavorful fare, Dive features local organic produce, seasonal seafood entrees and an array of creative salads, sandwiches, sangrias and cocktails. Nothing is reheated—everything is made to order. Available for lunch and early dinner, Dive is open Monday through Saturday, from 11am to 9pm.

Specialty: Coastal-inspired Fresh Yummies
3404 Rankin St, Dallas, 214.891.1700
dive-dallas.com

Photos by Catie Ronquillo

Photos by Catie Ronquillo

Ebony Peoples Events & Design

Dallas, Texas

Stylish. Glam. Exquisite.

Ebony Peoples Events & Design is an event planning and design boutique where traditional elegance meets modern glam! Whether you're planning an intimate shower for 20 people or an extravagant wedding for 200 people, Ebony's team will ensure that your event exudes personal style with exquisite detail and efficient orchestration.

Ebony Peoples-Wordlaw

Q&A

What do you like best about owning a business?
I absolutely *love* what I do! Day in and day out I have an opportunity to live out my dreams by helping others celebrate some of life's most precious moments.

Who is your role model or mentor?
My mommy, grandmother and great-grandmother are my role models. These strong and amazing women have always encouraged me to live life to the fullest and give thanks daily.

What is your motto or theme song?
"Give a girl the right shoes and she can conquer the world." —Marilyn Monroe

Specialties: Wedding and Event Planning, Event Design
214.702.2410, ebonypeoples.com
facebook.com/EbonyPeoplesEventsandDesign
Twitter: @ebonypeoples

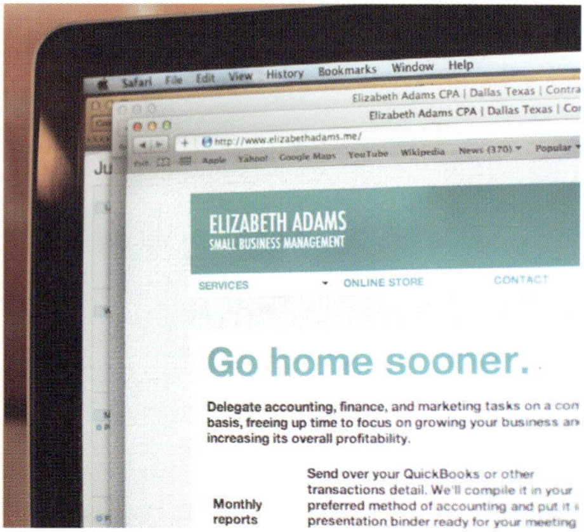

Q&A

What are your most popular products or services?
QuickBooks setup for new companies, creation of flexible spreadsheets for forecasting and business plans, Excel training, monthly social media management and employee recruitment via LinkedIn.

What tip would you give women who are starting a business?
Know your personality, strengths and interests. Connect with people who encourage, challenge and energize you to reach your goals.

What is your biggest fear?
Failure. But I refuse to let it get in my way!

Elizabeth Adams, CPA

Dallas, Texas

Practical. Insightful. Necessary.
Elizabeth Adams is a business consultant who provides accounting, finance and marketing services on a contract basis to local companies. She's a Texas CPA with Big Four audit experience, has degrees from SMU in accounting and advertising, and has a passion for small business.

Specialties: Small Business Accounting, Finance, Marketing
214.377.1150, elizabethadams.me
Twitter: @atypicalcpa, linkedin.com/in/adamselizabeth

Photos by Catie Ronquillo

Elle Parks

Dallas, Texas

Organic. Dreamy. Effortless.

Elle Parks is a commercial photographer with a passion for telling dreamy stories through the creative palette of her lens. She captures the delicate beauty of life, evoking mood-changing emotions with a simple charm and effortless vintage appeal. Her distinctive style is timeless.

Specialty: Storytelling through Photography
214.405.5331, elleparksphotography.com
Twitter: @elleparksphoto
linkedin.com/in/elleparksphotography

Photos by Elle Parks Photography

Elle Parks

Q&A

What are your most popular products or services?
Styled commercial shoots. With our background in the fashion industry, we design each shoot to be as unique as our clients.

What tip would you give women who are starting a business?
Never forget how smart and courageous you really are. Never compare yourself with anyone; comparison is the biggest joy stealer. Never be afraid to dream a little bigger.

What do you like best about owning a business?
I get to meet and work with so many amazing people every day! I am so blessed.

Q&A

What tip would you give women who are starting a business?
Get your name out there. Build a website, make business cards and go to as many networking events as possible. You are your biggest champion, so go spread the word!

What do you like best about owning a business?
Both the freedom and the responsibility that come with it. I have the flexibility to do what I want, but it requires attention to detail, efficiency and financial responsibility.

What motivates you on a daily basis?
Art is my passion; it is innate in me. I wake up energized every morning knowing that I get to pursue my lifelong dream of painting and creating art.

Ellis Art Gallery

Dallas, Texas

Modern. Expressive. Vibrant.
Native Texan Melissa Ellis specializes in spectacular, vivid abstract oil paintings, as well as bold yet delicate trees and flowers. Her sense of style is uniquely her own with her distinct color choices, fresh approach to the traditional and the intricate details of each painting. Melissa's work is available online, and she also accepts commissions for both residential and commercial spaces.

Portrait and top right photo by Matt & Julie Weddings

Faryn Clark

Q&A

What are your most popular products or services?
Our skincare program is really popular, and we offer services like facials, peels, microderm, dermaplaning, massage, airbrush tanning, waxing, body treatments, lash extensions, teeth whitening and makeup applications and lessons.

What is your biggest fear?
That I will get caught up in the business of life and not live in the moment. I don't want to blink and have it be too late to really *live*.

What is your motto or theme song?
"I alone cannot change the world, but I can cast a stone across the waters to create many ripples." —Mother Teresa

Facelogic Spa

Highland Park and University Park, Texas

Relaxing. Rejuvenating. Affordable.
Facelogic Spa, located in Park Cities, is a spa like no other. They offer customized facials, massage, airbrush tanning, face and body waxing, makeup, lash extensions, body treatments and so much more. With Facelogic's essential skincare program, you can save money with each and every treatment that you receive in the spa. Their expert aestheticians will give you treatments that provide relaxation and dramatic results.

Specialties: Skincare, Tanning, Waxing, Massage, Lash Extensions
Facelogic Spa: 4518 Lovers Ln, Dallas
214.696.3223, dallas.facelogicspa.com
facebook.com/FacelogicHighlandPark
Twitter: @FacelogicHP

Photos by Claire McCormack

Fairy Godmother Bridal Agency

Dallas, Texas

Beautiful. Flexible. Professional.

The first time someone called her a Fairy Godmother was over 15 years ago. It started like it should, with a wish for something that didn't already exist. Mo Bowers has assembled an elite team that delivers more than pretty hair and makeup for that most memorable day, such as prom or an anniversary, in the boudoir, or for head shots. The artists are talented yet calming, patient and creative!

Photos by Kelly Rucker Photography, Celina Gomez and F8 Studios

Q&A

What tip would you give women who are starting a business?
Have a business plan! When you're in the thick of it, five years or so, you may need to remind yourself why you wanted this so much.

Who is your role model or mentor?
Madonna (she had a business plan by the way!), Tim (my best friend) and my mom.

What place inspires you?
Fabric stores and thrift shops. I love transformation. I see the endless possibilities everywhere around me!

What do you CRAVE?
More women sharing in the cycle of inspiration, creativity and dreams coming true.

Photos by Katie Cassidy Photography

Fashion Fix Style

Dallas, Texas

Efficient. Fun. Transformative.
Fashion Fix Style will get you out of your wardrobe rut and help define your self-image and personal style. Fashion Fix Style is a full-service wardrobe consulting firm that provides wardrobe solutions for professional women and men, celebrities, publications and fashion companies. Services include personal shopping, closet cleanse, photo shoot styling, runway styling, event styling, costume design and public speaking.

Porsche Montgomery

Q&A

What tip would you give women who are starting a business?
Give yourself a chance to be successful, it takes time to grow your business. It is important to constantly remind yourself of the mission and vision of your business.

What do you like best about owning a business?
Making an impact on my clients' lives and the flexibility. It's an amazing feeling when you have the option to pursue your dreams and do what you love!

What motivates you on a daily basis?
My love for fashion and my clients. We have such a great time together, shopping and purging their closets; I love making the connections and positively affecting their self-image.

Specialty: Personal Styling
702.416.0504, fashionfixstyle.com
facebook.com/FashionFixStyle
Twitter: @FashionFixStyle

Q&A

What tip would you give women who are starting a business?
Start small and expand slowly.

What do you like best about owning a business?
The freedom of creativity. And I can change something immediately. No waiting on anyone else to make a decision.

How do you relax?
I read travel and cooking periodicals.

What place inspires you?
Italy... simple, simple food exquisitely prepared.

What motivates you on a daily basis?
Putting out the best product possible every day!

The Festive Kitchen

Highland Park, Dallas, and Richardson, Texas

Delicious. Recognizable. Handcrafted

The Festive Kitchen provides full-service catering for any event: wedding, corporate or social. Visit one of their stores for food for dinner tonight or hors d'oeuvres and desserts for weekend company. All food is of the highest quality, handcrafted and made with pure ingredients. Just like you would make it yourself... if you had the time!

This page: left photo by Brittany Nicole, right photo by Dave Edmonson, opposite page: portrait by Mark Moore, lower photos by Sandy Korem

Oluremi Sano

Q&A

What tip would you give women who are starting a business?
Have a business plan! Be true to your authentic self, while growing your business. And be wise about your personal and professional associations!

What are your most popular products or services?
Zumba is one of the most explosive fitness programs out today, and Fihankra Dance & Fitness Studio boasts the best of the best in terms of instructors!

How do you relax?
By spending time with close friends or taking a hot bath with Epsom salts and essential oils.

What place inspires you?
The library!

Fihankra Dance & Fitness Studio

Historic Deep Ellum, Dallas

Fun. Healthy. Rewarding.

Fihankra Dance & Fitness Studio is one of Dallas's premier studios for dance and fitness! It has one of the largest varieties of classes, including Zumba, salsa, African dance, cardio kickboxing, yoga, pole fitness, adult hip-hop, ballet, burlesque and more! Fihankra Dance Studio will be growing to include a beautiful ballroom location in Deep Ellum, as well as two new satellite locations in Duncanville and Lancaster!

Photos by Tamyra Campbell, except portrait

The Film Firm

Dallas, Texas

Engaging. Inspiring. Authentic.

The Film Firm is a small boutique film house. They specialize in short stories, micro documentaries, unique small business and corporate video profiles, and commercial campaigns. They have a cinematic style and artistic approach that engages and inspires. Driven by story, with close attention to detail, every video is handcrafted to deliver a powerful message that captivates a broad audience.

Specialty: Film and Video Media Production
972.900.9467, TheFilmFirm.com
Twitter: @filmfirmUS, linkedin.com/in/JanRuley

Q&A

What are your most popular products or services?
We believe the story of a business or an individual is their best marketing tool. Our Long Story Short package is a 2–3 minute handcrafted video portrait that works for any business.

What tip would you give women who are starting a business?
Find something that you really enjoy doing so that work doesn't feel like work. Don't put it off. If you think you'll get around to it someday, someday may never come.

How do you relax?
I've always loved the ocean; that's where I first made an impact through film. Diving, to me, is the most relaxing and peaceful way to spend a day.

Fit Family Health

Dallas, Texas

Functional. Inspirational. Holistic.
Brig offers local boot camps, private PT sessions and online coaching. Her experience as a certified personal trainer, certified sports nutritionist and P90X Certified Team Beachbody Coach helps Brig empower her clients to reach their fitness goals. Her purpose is to help others see that anything is possible "as long as you commit, believe and are willing to let me help you reach your goals!"

Specialties: Weight Loss, Nutrition, Workout Programs, Support
469.396.8417, fitfamilyhealth.com
facebook.com/brigid.wollack
Twitter: @fitfamilyhealth

Photos by Elle Parks Photography

Q&A

What tip would you give women who are starting a business?
When the Holy Spirit calls, jump in! We are a collection of countless experiences, choices, mistakes and victories—together we can reach our greatest successes.

What do you like best about owning a business?
The opportunity to help others reach wellness goals, create positive change, achieve balance, understand nutrition and apply the keys to exercise fuels my passion and life-song.

What do you CRAVE?
A commitment to perseverance, courage and diligence from everyone I work with.

Julie Porter

Q&A

What are your most popular products or services?
Branding, strategy and development, marketing, media planning, message mapping, creative advertising, social media and public relations.

What tip would you give women who are starting a business?
Assemble a trusted advisory council composed of people who are expert in areas you are not. Value them, utilize them, celebrate them. They will be your most avid cheerleaders.

What do you like best about owning a business?
Not working for "the man," our flexible work culture and the fact that I get to choose my clients and my team—no energy vampires allowed!

Specialties: Branding, Marketing, Advertising, Social Media
214.704.3465, itsfrontporch.com, Twitter: @juliedporter01
facebook.com/FrontPorchMktg, linkedin.com/in/juliedporter

Front Porch Marketing

Dallas, Texas

Collaborative. Social. Rockin'.

Front Porch Marketing specializes in branding successful businesses. It's not just a logo. It's a unique emotional connection with the customer. If your current branding isn't working or you don't know where to start marketing, contact the folks at Front Porch Marketing and let them help!

Photos by Katie Cassidy Photography

Frontier Paper Co.

Dallas, Texas

Fresh. Custom. Distinctive.

Frontier Paper Co. designs and creates custom wedding invitations with a decidedly fresh perspective on a couple's individual style. Allison and Libby work with each client, bringing an inspired concept to reality on paper. Offering a range of printing mediums, they specialize in letterpress suites that lean toward the natural and whimsical. These are invitations that you're sad to unpin from your bulletin board.

Specialty: Invitation Design
frontierpapercompany.com

Photos by Natalie Pitts

Libby Smith and Allison Dowell

Q&A

What are your most popular products or services?
Custom-designed wedding invitation suites—wedding invitations, save the dates, rehearsal dinner invitations, programs, thank-you notes and all the coordinating paper pieces that a couple needs.

What tip would you give women who are starting a business?
Don't hesitate to shift goals/responsibilities. It takes time to determine how everyone's strengths will best be used to the fullest.

What do you like best about owning a business?
It's thrilling to bring a client's vague design notions to fruition.

Frosted Pink Cake Company

Mansfield, Texas

Nostalgic. Tasty. Irresistible.

Frosted Pink Cake is an exclusive cake company in Mansfield, specializing in everything cake: custom cakes, wedding cakes, cupcakes and cake truffles! They start every morning with pure Madagascar Bourbon vanillas, luscious chocolates, fresh eggs and dairy that blend together to create delectable cakes, cupcakes and creamy frostings. Their creations are baked in small batches in their shop to ensure the cakes are at their finest.

Specialties: Custom Cakes, Cupcakes and Cake Truffles
117 N Main St, Ste 200, Mansfield, 817.473.7465
frostedpinkcake.com, Twitter: @frostedpinkcake
facebook.com/frostedpinkcakecompany

Photos by Catie Ronquillo, except lower middle photo

Q&A

What are your most popular products or services?
Customers love our cupcakes! Cupcakes are our creative opportunity to mix up exciting and tasty flavors. Cupcakes are the perfect indulgence but small enough to be guilt-free.

How do you relax?
Time with my family, watching movies, and my newest addiction: the gym!

What tip would you give women who are starting a business?
Know your business, know your product and love what you do. When you love what you do, your customers will too.

What do you CRAVE?
Everything sweet, and a vacation!

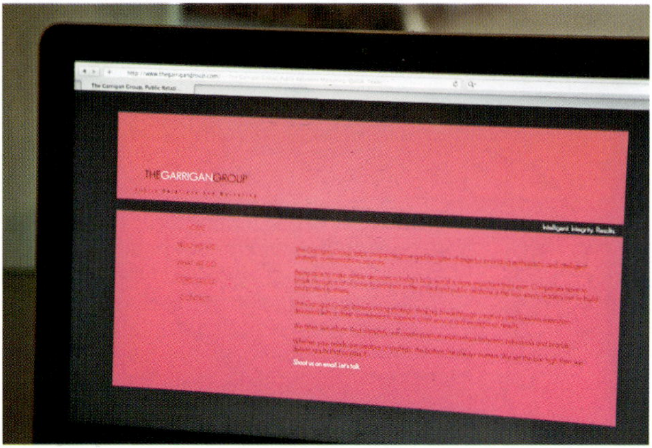

Courtney Garrigan Milburn

Q&A

What do you like best about owning a business?
The independence to make things happen.

What place inspires you?
The view from my desk. It is positioned so that I can see out onto the treetops outside my balcony doors. It's really peaceful.

What tip would you give women who are starting a business?
Do what you love, and then excel at it.

How do you relax?
I certainly love a good nap! But spending downtime with my girlfriends really helps me relax.

What is your motto or theme song?
Always do the next right thing.

The Garrigan Group

Dallas, Texas

Insightful. Enthusiastic. Strategic.

The Garrigan Group works with a select clientele to grow and navigate change by providing intelligent strategic communications services. Based on more than 25 years of experience in public relations and marketing, The Garrigan Group helps clients reach goals and increase revenue by offering a variety of PR services that build brand image and develop credibility.

Specialties: PR, Marketing, Strategic Planning
214.282.3735, thegarrigangroup.com

Photos by Katie Cassidy Photography

Get Noticed Boutique

Richardson, Texas

Enjoyable. Feminine. Sophisticated.

Get Noticed Boutique (GNB) is a ladies' specialty store always full of clothing, shoes, cowgirl boots, accessories and SPANX. At GNB you will find everything you need for your next special event, date night, girls' night out, or if you just want to look great going to the grocery store. With your personal shopping experience, you will walk away with a complete look.

Specialty: Personalized Fashion Styling
635 W Campbell Rd, Ste 308, Richardson
972.664.9551, getnoticedboutique.com

Photos by Morgan Jordan Photography

Q&A

What tip would you give women who are starting a business?
Your business is who you hire; make sure that your staff is a reflection of integrity. Support your community; that is where your business comes from. Remain passionate about your business.

What motivates you on a daily basis?
I am motivated by my family that I have been blessed with. My customers: I love giving them unrestricted service; I am only a phone call or text away!

What is your motto or theme song?
"Life is too short to blend in."
—Paris Hilton. Your appearance is a snapshot of who you are.

What is your biggest fear?
I don't live in fear; that will defeat you.

Q&A

What are your most popular products or services?
h design is sought out primarily for excellent 3-D virtual architectural and construction modeling as well as creative, custom invites and thank-you cards for events.

What tip would you give women who are starting a business?
Give yourself a considerable measure of grace. And be patient as you work to implement your big ideas. Marketing is nothing without careful, deliberate development.

What motivates you on a daily basis?
I strive every day to be a better wife, mother and person than I am capable of being today.

h design and Cole London

Dallas, Texas

Visual. Modern. Handcrafted.
h design provides modern, sustainable, innovative design solutions for architectural and virtual design and construction needs for both commercial and residential sectors. h design also has a strong portfolio of graphic design services including stationery design, logos and branding for business owners and individuals. The company's subsidiary, Cole London, is a photography-inspired stationery line. The stationery is made using a unique handcrafted, then photographed, then printed process.

Specialties: Architectural Design, Graphic Design

h design: 214.727.6650, harperdesignprojects.com
facebook.com/harperdesignprojects, Twitter: @hdesignbuzz

Cole London: 214.727.6650, colelondonpaper.com
facebook.com/ColeLondonPaper, Twitter: @ColeLondonPaper

linkedin.com/in/sarahharper

Photos by Kelly Rucker Photography

Photos by Kelly Rucker Photography

Harmony Marketing

Dallas, Texas

Educational. Engaging. Relevant.

Harmony Marketing works with small to medium-sized businesses building their email marketing strategy and guiding their social media campaigns. Whether clients attend a class on email marketing or social media or prefer to work one-on-one, Harmony Marketing is able to show small-business owners how to utilize these low-cost tools to build connections and grow their business.

Q&A

What are your most popular products or services?
Our email marketing classes get such a positive response. They inspire people who don't know where to begin. Once they get going, clients understand the relevance and effectiveness of email marketing.

What tip would you give women who are starting a business?
Find your groove. Without a routine of some sort, you can get overwhelmed easily. And don't limit yourself!

What is your motto or theme song?
"Whether you think you can or think you can't, you're right." —Henry Ford. This is so true in life and in business.

What place inspires you?
The ocean is awe-inspiring. Spending time near the water always rejuvenates my soul and my mind.

Rosie Vann-Dalton and Sande Brandt

Q&A

What are your most popular products or services?

Our most popular service is our girlfriend shopping parties. Women love to invite girlfriends, sip "Cantinis" and share laughs while shopping. Popular designers include Sky, Level 99 and Union of Angels.

What tip would you give women who are starting a business?

Feel passionately about your concept. Test it, play devil's advocate, ask yourself and others you trust tough questions and be open to constructive criticism. Your research strengthens your passion.

What do you like best about owning a business?

We both feel a deep sense of pride that we were able to dream this concept into reality, and we get to go to a party every day in our business!

High Maintenance "Couture in a Can"

Dallas, Texas

Fashionable. Mobile. Convenient.
High Maintenance "Couture in a Can" offers a unique wardrobe experience to all women with their 1977 converted Airstream. Curbside celebrity styling is tailored to both women who love to shop or women who simply need to "check it off the list." High Maintenance features fashionably relevant designers not saturated in DFW and dresses women throughout their busy days. Stress-free shopping at its best!

Hitched Events

Dallas, Texas

Personalized. Organized. Attentive.

Hitched Events is a boutique event-management company focused on the planning and execution of modern weddings and other celebratory events in the Dallas–Fort Worth area. From an intimate wedding for 40 people to a gala for 400 people, Hitched Events can handle all the details, allowing clients to fully relax and enjoy the celebration. Owner Kimberly Rhodes has an eye for detail and passion for perfection.

Specialty: Wedding and Event Planning
214.699.9933, hitched-events.com
facebook.com/HitchedEvents, Twitter: @HitchedDallas

Photos by Katie Cassidy Photography

Q&A

What is your motto or theme song?
I recently put a poster up in my office that says, "Everybody that is a somebody at one time was a nobody. Dream big!"

What tip would you give women who are starting a business?
Find a way to pay yourself regularly, even if it's a tiny amount at first. There's something mentally rewarding and empowering about writing yourself a paycheck. You've earned it!

What place inspires you?
The ocean. My husband and I are certified scuba divers, and there's nothing like being 70 feet underwater to make you realize the world is a pretty amazing, awe-inspiring place.

Photos by Natalie Pits, portrait (opposite page) by Carl Studna

Humanistic Consulting

Dallas, Texas

Energetic. Informative. Valuable.

Humanistic Consulting enables business owners to work on their business as opposed to in their business so that they can focus on their key drivers such as enhancing revenue, driving profitability and thwarting competition. Their goal is to make businesses successful by formulating strategies and creating HR policies and practices for recruiting, training and development, legal compliance, employee relations, compensation, benefits, succession planning and retention programs.

Q&A

What tip would you give women who are starting a business?
Identify your purpose or mission, your company values and your brand promise. When you have a challenging day, go back to your purpose to keep you focused and grounded.

What do you like best about owning a business?
I love the variety. Every day is a new challenge with constant learning. I also love bringing solutions to my clients and helping them grow their business.

How do you relax?
I practice power yoga. It brings me clarity, energy and a sense of calm. I also try to laugh every day. There is humor everywhere when you look for it.

Specialties: HR Outsourcing, HR Products, Training, Speaking
469.766.6110, humanisticconsulting.com
ihatehrbut.com, Twitter: @glennahecht
linkedin.com/in/glennahecht

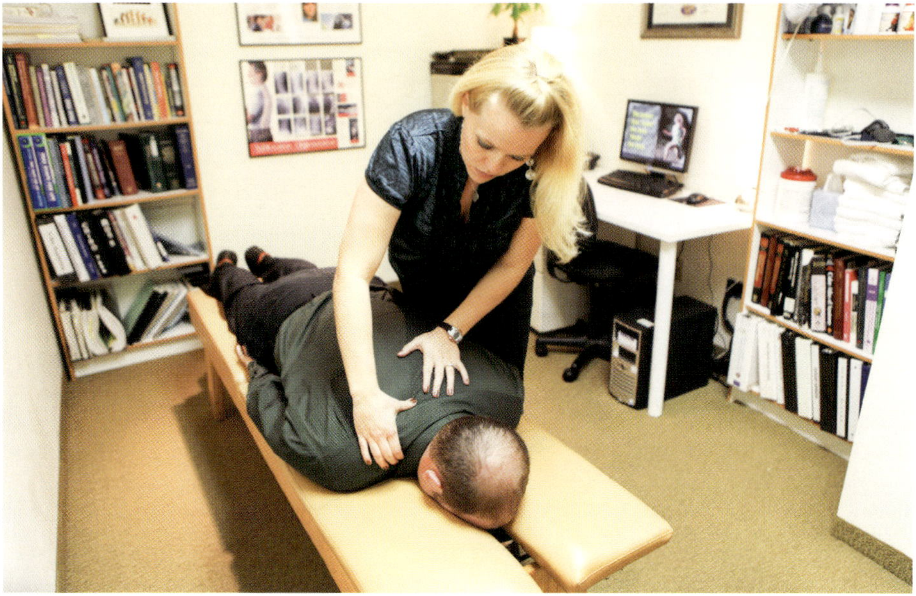

Photos by Claire McCormack

Inwood Chiropractic Center

Park Cities, Dallas

Honest. Encouraging. Energetic.

At Inwood Chiropractic Center, Dr. Caley strives for excellence through superior patient treatment, education and satisfaction. The clinic offers multiple treatments to customize each patient's optimal health plan. Dr. Caley listens to each patient and helps them achieve their health and wellness goals naturally, effectively, and most importantly, without the use of medications that tend to cover the symptom and not treat the problem.

Q&A

What tip would you give women who are starting a business?
Never give up, every day has its ups and downs, but the roller coaster is what makes life fun!

What do you like best about owning a business?
The flexibility of working my own hours and knowing you can be as successful as you want to be.

What motivates you on a daily basis?
Seeing my patients achieve optimal health and function naturally, as well as educating them to live a healthier, wellness-based lifestyle.

What is your motto or theme song?
"Be the change you wish to see in the world." —Gandhi

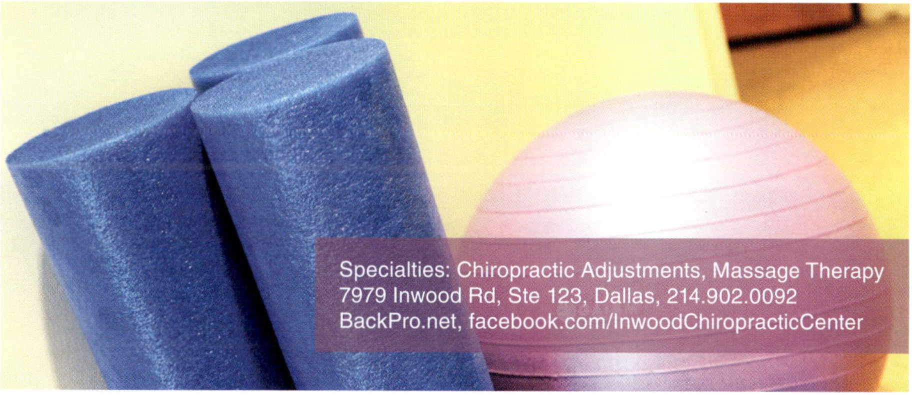

Q&A

What tip would you give women who are starting a business?
Don't be afraid to ask questions. Get out there and talk to people. Networking groups, friends, social networks like Facebook and Twitter. Be open and share your ideas.

What place inspires you?
I love going to the nursery and seeing all the beautiful plants. Some girls go crazy over shoes; I go nuts over plants! I want one of everything!

What do you CRAVE?
Beautiful environments that fill me with joy, peacefulness and serenity. There is nothing more satisfying than truly experiencing the beauty and complexity of nature!

JDS Design

Dallas, Texas

Imaginative. Energetic. Expressive.

JDS Design provides professional landscape design and consulting as well as project management of residential landscape installations. Julie Simons has a passion for creating unique, functional and beautiful landscape exteriors that reflect and embody her clients' desires, needs and personal tastes. Energetic, hands-on and extremely knowledgeable, Julie turns visions into reality in gardens throughout the Dallas area.

Specialty: Residential Landscape Design
214.394.2281, jdsdesign.biz, Twitter: @juliedsimons

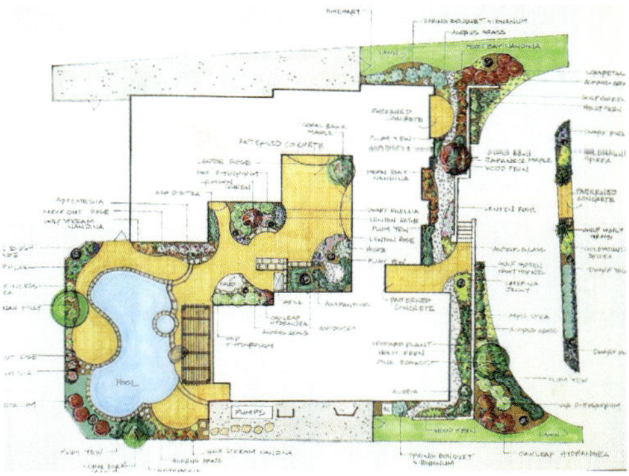

Photos by Scarlet Barksdale Photography

Jenn Sprinkle Creative

Dallas, Texas

Modern. Creative. Functional.
Jenn Sprinkle Creative is in the business of taking your business from fine to fabulous through branding and creative strategy. Jenn's passion for entrepreneurs pours into every branding and design project she does, encouraging business owners along the way. This passion has also inspired a new product line of fashionable and functional office products, stationery and textiles to create inspired work spaces for inspired work.

Specialties: Branding, Design, Printing, Stationery and Gifts
817.233.4724, jennsprinkle.com
Twitter: @jenn_sprinkle
facebook.com/JennSprinkleCreative

Photos by Elle Parks Photography, except lower left photo by Claire McCormack

Jenn Sprinkle

Q&A

What are your most popular products or services?
We work a lot with small businesses to refresh their brand or launch a new one. Our Multitasker Jotter and fashionable iPhone cases are a favorite among our customers!

What do you like best about owning a business?
The community of dreamers. I love the passion that is behind every business owner, and I love sharing in that community. It's so inspiring.

What is your motto or theme song?
I live by three mottoes: meetings are most effective over chips and salsa; I can't do my job without cool office supplies; and my job is to make people smile.

Jordan Filloon

Q&A

What tip would you give women who are starting a business?

Devise a clear plan of what you want to do and how you intend to do it, and stick with it. Without a game plan you will get nowhere. Keep your eye on the prize!

What motivates you on a daily basis?

My kids. I do it all for them. Making my clients happy and ensuring they leave my chair looking and feeling amazing is also deeply gratifying for me.

Who is your role model or mentor?

My mom and my baby sister. Jennifer Lopez also inspires me because she came from very humble beginnings and now does it all.

How do you relax?

As a Pisces I love being around water, so poolside or at the beach are where I'm happiest. A cocktail, good music and friends complete the picture!

Jordan Filloon

Addison, Texas

Trendy. Creative. Chic.

Jordan Filloon is a versatile stylist with a firm foundation of hair knowledge and over a decade of experience in the industry. Her skills quickly propelled her to the top of her field as an educator and she now showcases her talents styling high-fashion shoots with some of the area's top photographers, including a recent cover for Atlanta-based lifestyle magazine *Fenuxe*. From a simple blowout to on-location wedding services—whether it's classic or cutting edge—Jordan is an expert at tailoring a client's style to fit their needs, and her keen eye for color and style means you'll always leave her chair feeling like a million bucks.

Specialties: Haircuts and Color for Men and Women
By appointment: 5402 Arapaho Rd, Ste 41, Dallas
972.979.8813, jordanfilloon.com
jordan@jordanfilloon.com
facebook.com/jordandoesmyhair

Photos by Kelly Rucker Photography

Julep

Plano, Texas

Sophisticated. Simplistic. Elegant.

Julep's owner, Cheryl McDonald, edits numerous collections and assembles a wardrobe any woman would desire to have in her closet today. Julep reflects the sophisticated but casual ease of Cheryl's California home, specializing in soft, luxurious fabrics and styles. Along with clothing, Julep offers a collection of jewelry—many pieces from local designers, handbags and scarves, as well as an apothecary and home decor.

Photos by Elle Parks Photography, except lower right photo (this page) and lower left photo (opposite page)

Specialties: Women's Clothing and Accessories
Shops at Legacy: 7161 Bishop Road G3, Plano
877.585.3763, www.julep.me, Twitter: @Julepme
facebook.com/JulepMe

Q&A

What are your most popular products or services?
Soft luxurious fabrics such as silk chiffon, cashmere and cotton. Michael Stars, Susana Monaco, Fifteen Twenty and 360 Sweater. Jewelry designers LeighElena, Deborah Gaspar and Sarah Briggs.

What motivates you on a daily basis?
The pace of fashion, its constant change and diversity, and the challenge to create a fashion environment for my customer that is relevant today.

What do you CRAVE?
A smile. It's so simple but so powerful!

Katie Cassidy Photography

Dallas, Texas

Photojournalistic. Beautiful. Heartfelt.
Katie Cassidy Photography specializes in wedding coverage from the engagement session, bridals, rehearsal, wedding day and day after to even trashing the dress! Combining their artistic talents and love for storytelling to capture candids, casual portraits, fun accidents, sweet happenings and heartfelt details, Katie Cassidy Photography strives to document your wedding journey in a timeless manner, filled with love, beauty, emotion and merriment!

Photos by Katie Cassidy Photography, except portrait by Kelly Rucker Photography

Q&A

What are your most popular products or services?
Our complete wedding package, which includes an engagement session, all-day coverage, two shooters, images, online gallery and custom albums.

What is your motto or theme song?
"Here Comes the Sun" by The Beatles. No matter what situation you are going through, the sun will always shine.

What do you CRAVE?
DIY projects. The need to be creative and produce something pretty gets me every time!

What motivates you on a daily basis?
My family. They are the drive behind everything I do.

Kelly Rucker Photography

Dallas, Texas

Photos by Kelly Rucker Photography

Modern. Stylish. Romantic.
Kelly Rucker is a wedding and portrait photographer based in Dallas. Her work is modern and stylish, with an editorial appeal. Her goals are to create the images and products that you will cherish for a lifetime and to provide an exceptional photography experience.

Specialty: Wedding and Portrait Photography
512.300.3786, kellyrucker.com
Twitter: @kelrucker
facebook.com/KellyRuckerPhotography

Q&A

What are your most popular products or services?
Two of our biggest clients are brides and moms. We provide wedding coverage including engagements, bridals and boudoir for brides as well as maternity days and newborn moments for moms.

What motivates you on a daily basis?
My life list! Several years ago I created a list of all the things I wanted to accomplish in life. It reminds me to pursue my dreams daily.

What is your motto or theme song?
A lyric that gives me great perspective: "Whatever may pass and whatever lies before me, let me be singing when the evening comes."

Kelly Bennett

Q&A

What tip would you give women who are starting a business?
Be as tenacious as a bulldog! If you believe in your product and yourself, you will create amazing things!

What do you like best about owning a business?
I don't report to anyone, and nobody reports to me... love the autonomy!

What motivates you on a daily basis?
Exercise. I would go crazy without it!

What place inspires you and why?
Volunteering at Genesis Women's Shelter. Those women and children do more for me than I could ever do for them. They embody the word *strength*.

Kelly Von Sassypants

Dallas, Texas

Whimsical. Personalized. Authentic.

Kelly brings to the table an entrepreneurial passion that combines the art of writing, public speaking and her love for empowering others to put their best foot forward! She holds a B.A. in Education from the University of Texas at Austin, and her background includes teaching (both local and international), curriculum development, public speaking, creative writing, technical writing and consulting for nonprofits.

Photos by Catie Ronquillo

Kim Rozell Makeup Design

Dallas, Texas

Timeless. Flawless. Modern.

Kim Rozell's signature look of timeless, classic beauty with a modern approach has won her local and national recognition with credits in *Time*, *People*, *Allure*, *Town & Country* and on CNN, *Oprah* and *20/20*. Kim's artistry and personal warmth have made her a favorite with models, celebrities and blushing brides. *Town & Country* says, "When planning the perfect wedding, call Kim Rozell."

Q&A

What tip would you give women who are starting a business?
Keep it simple. Keep overhead down. Architect and designer Mies van der Rohe said it best, "Less is more." That's my philosophy when applying makeup and in business.

Who is your role model or mentor?
My mother. She has impeccable taste, style and character. She worked as a model for Neiman Marcus when she was young, and I followed her into the fashion world.

What place inspires you?
Paris. The city of lights is where I trained as a makeup artist, and it is the place where so much in the fashion world begins.

Kim Truman

Q&A

What tip would you give women who are starting a business?
Embrace the journey. Never let someone else's "no" stop you from pursuing your own vision. Be persistent with a structured plan. Love what you do—your passion will shine!

What motivates you on a daily basis?
Life! My son! To create a legacy to help others spread love and embrace their purpose.

Who is your role model or mentor?
My parents. Both are incredible people who taught me that success comes from the person you are within and how you treat others. They instilled in me character and integrity. Live with love and purpose, and help others.

KimTrumanFitness

Dallas, Texas

Compassionate. Determined. Energetic.

Kim Truman is a fitness instructor, personal trainer, lifestyle coach and contributing writer to multiple magazines. Zealous about life, Kim's love of people comes through from watching her infectious energy when teaching or helping one-on-one, motivating and connecting people in a challenging atmosphere. As a personal trainer and life coach, she strives to empower her clients, show them purpose in life and teach them how to make healthy choices both physically and emotionally.

Specialties: Group and Personal Training, Life Coaching, Writing
214.577.7441, kimtrumanfitness.com
facebook.com/kimtrumanfitness
Twitter: @IfnotnowwhenKT

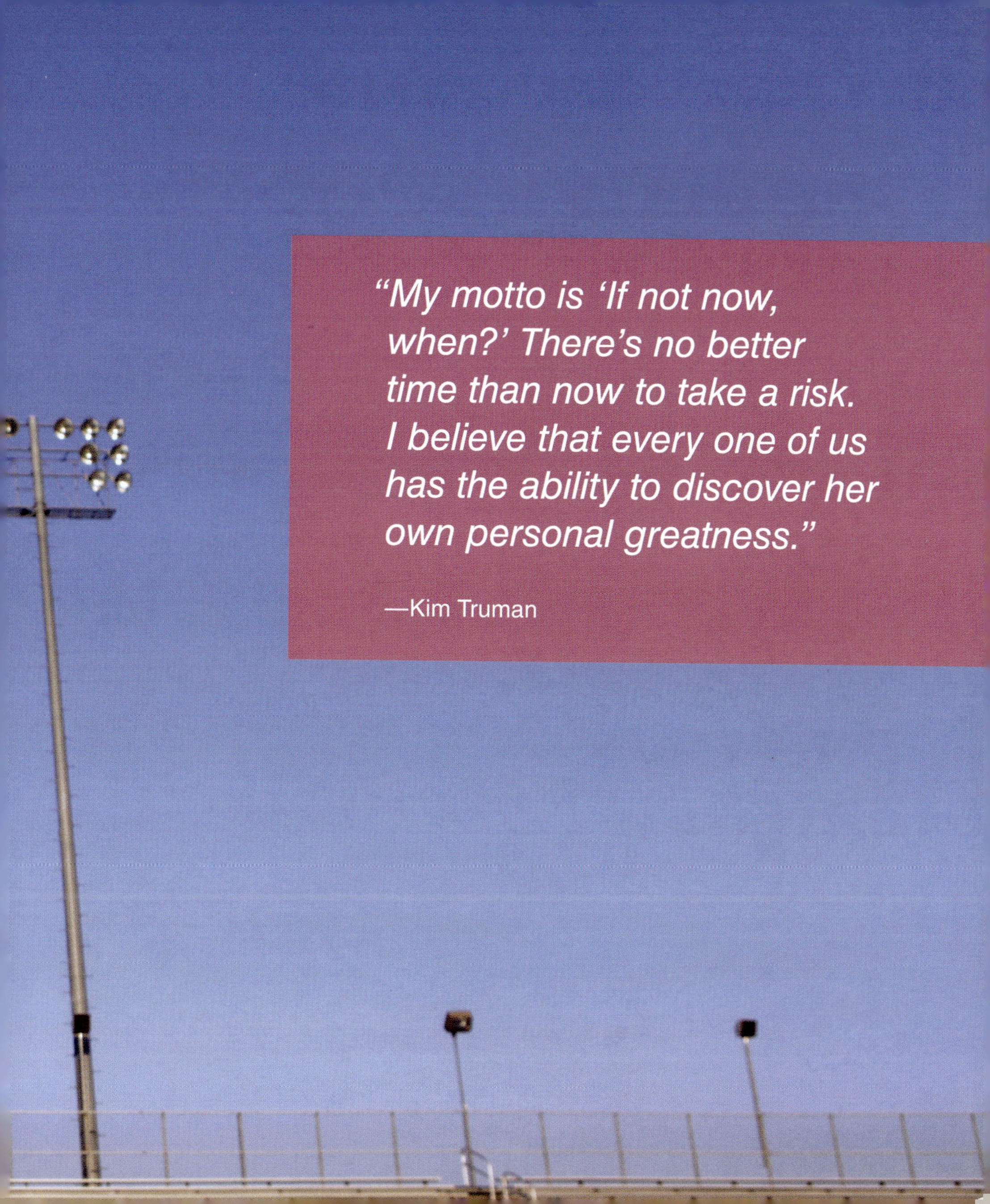

"My motto is 'If not now, when?' There's no better time than now to take a risk. I believe that every one of us has the ability to discover her own personal greatness."

—Kim Truman

Q&A

What are your most popular products or services?
Ultrasounds (both gender and 3-D/4-D), Perfect Pregnancy Massage, Get That Glow Facial and our yummy Chocolate Cherry Pedicure!

What tip would you give women who are starting a business?
Find something that you love and are passionate about. Know your market and competition. Provide great customer service and make sure your employees follow suit.

Who is your role model or mentor?
My mother. She was the strongest woman I knew, and she instilled in me the drive to work hard to get ahead in life and be an independent woman.

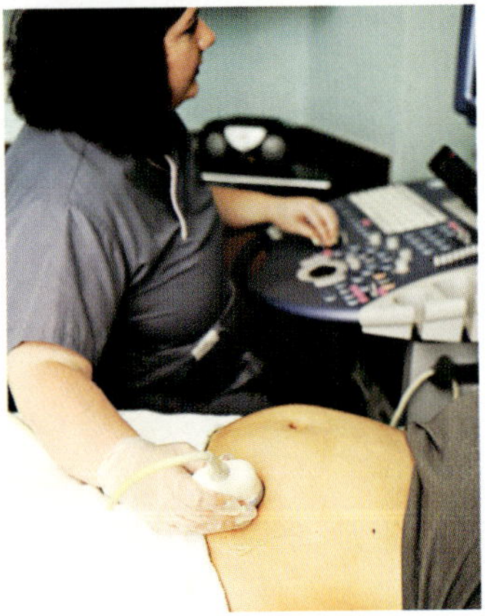

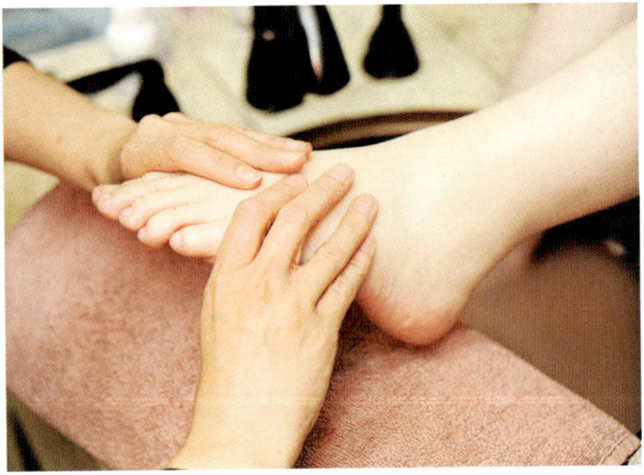

La Bella Belly

Pregnancy Spa & Ultrasound Center

Rockwall, Texas

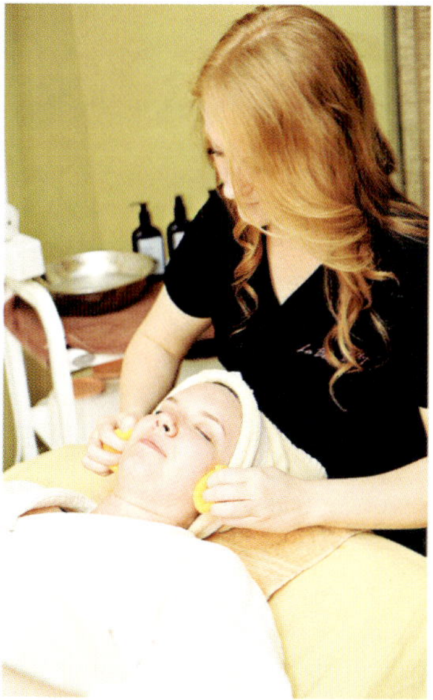

Relaxing. Exciting. Fun.
La Bella Belly specializes in meeting the unique and ever-changing needs of pregnant women or any mom! Their relaxing services are designed to treat all areas of concern safely and give you the pampering you deserve. Find out the gender or see baby's face for the first time in the large Ultrasound Center, which accommodates the entire family.

Specialties: Ultrasounds, Massage, Facials, Pedicures
By appointment: 3100 Ridge Road, Rockwall, 972.772.7212
labellabelly.com, facebook.com/labellabelly

Photos by Kelly Rucker Photography

The Lash Lounge

Dallas, Texas

Glamorous. Unique. Addictive.

The Lash Lounge is Texas's first eyelash-dedicated salon and the first eyelash salon franchise in the nation. Their specialty is the expert application of gorgeous semipermanent eyelash extensions. They also offer other eye-enhancing services that lend to providing a low-maintenance beauty routine, an exclusive cosmetics line and a trendy boutique. The Lash Lounge currently has seven locations throughout Texas and continues to expand.

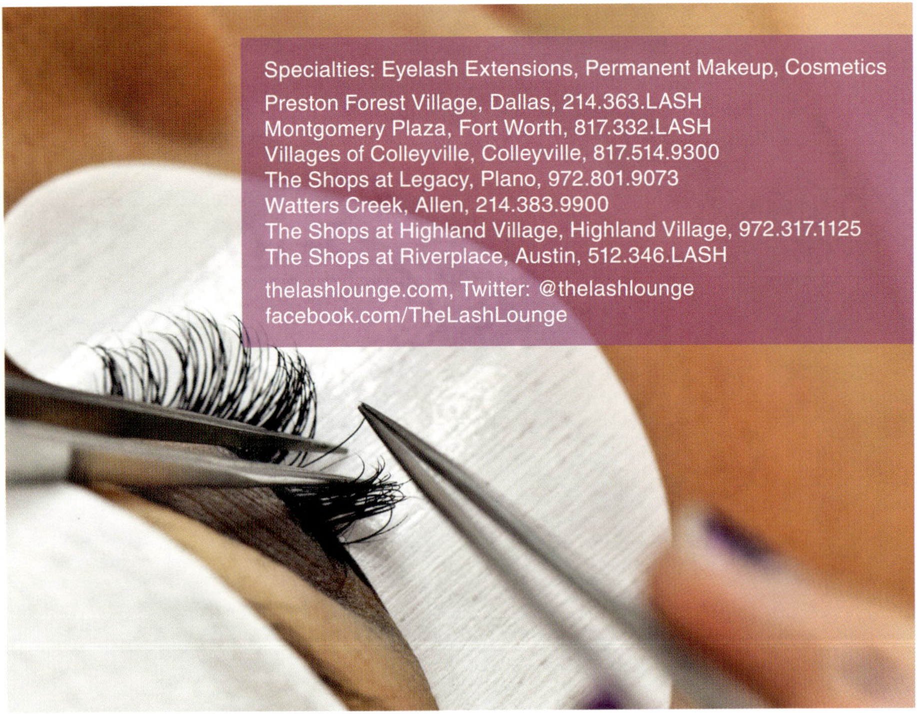

Specialties: Eyelash Extensions, Permanent Makeup, Cosmetics

Preston Forest Village, Dallas, 214.363.LASH
Montgomery Plaza, Fort Worth, 817.332.LASH
Villages of Colleyville, Colleyville, 817.514.9300
The Shops at Legacy, Plano, 972.801.9073
Watters Creek, Allen, 214.383.9900
The Shops at Highland Village, Highland Village, 972.317.1125
The Shops at Riverplace, Austin, 512.346.LASH

thelashlounge.com, Twitter: @thelashlounge
facebook.com/TheLashLounge

Photos by Katie Cassidy Photography

Anna Phillips

Q&A

What tip would you give women who are starting a business?
Create a business plan with thoughtful detail about how you will run your business when it flourishes and also when times are slow. This will prepare you for everything.

What is your motto or theme song?
"Give more than what is expected, and do it with a gracious heart." This has always been my philosophy on how we treat our clients.

What is your biggest fear?
Failure. I have so many people depending on me, and that is what drives me to work so hard to build a successful business.

Photos by Kelly Rucker Photography

LaurieGrace Coaching LLC

Dallas, Texas

Creative. Practical. Collaborative.

LaurieGrace Bouldin is a professional speaker, a credentialed coach and a relationship guru! She works with clients who want to strategically build collaboration so that they are achieving results like never before... personally and professionally. From Brainy Truths to Gender Smarts, LaurieGrace shares how we can develop "The Art of Relationship-ing" and begin creating extraordinary relationships. The key? It all starts with you.

Q&A

What tip would you give women who are starting a business?
Relationships are your greatest assets. They are the conduits that help you achieve any level of success that you'll ever have. Taking great care of them is essential.

What do you like best about owning a business?
I love being able to work from a center of passion and belief in what's possible. Achieving new results with like-minded clients is exhilarating. Together, we create change.

What is your motto or theme song?
"May you live all the days of your life." —Jonathan Swift

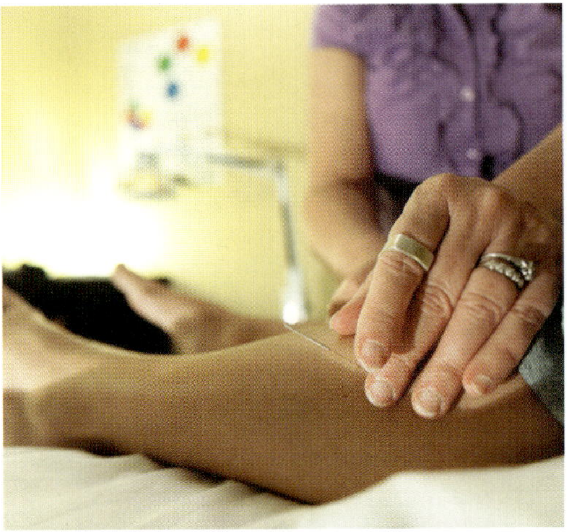

Q&A

What are your most popular products or services?
Our Be Well Circle membership with health coaching, massage, therapy, acupuncture and chiropractic care allows our clients to combine these services as needed each month to support their health goals.

What tip would you give women who are starting a business?
When you become an entrepreneur, you make sacrifices. If your business is your passion, you can thrive while experiencing the most awe-inspiring process of bringing your vision to life.

What is your motto or theme song?
"Be the change you wish to see in the world." —Gandhi

Living Well Health & Wellness Center

North Dallas

Innovative. Empowering. Compassionate.
Living Well Health & Wellness Center is the most comprehensive, integrative functional medicine center in the Metroplex. Living Well Health & Wellness Center recognizes that stress, relationships, lifestyle and spirituality are all part of your health. They combine medicine, nutrition, acupuncture, chiropractic, massage, therapy, energy medicine, biofeedback and professional organizing under one roof to help their clients in all areas of their life so that they can live, feel and be well.

Specialties: Health Care, Self Care, Nutrition, Bodywork
14330 Midway Road, Building 1, Ste 121, Dallas, 972.930.0260
livingwelldallas.com, Twitter: @livingwelldfw
facebook.com/livingwelldallas
bettymurray.com, Twitter: @bettymurray
facebook.com/bettymurray, linkedin.com/in/bettymurray

Photos by Matt & Julie Weddings

Cassy Zobel

Q&A

What tip would you give women who are starting a business?
If you've found your passion, follow it. Be prepared for long hours, lots of hard work, wearing many hats, and the joy that comes from doing something you absolutely love!

What is your motto or theme song?
Live your life so that when you're on your deathbed you have no reason to ask yourself that awful two-word question, "What if?"

What place inspires you?
The most inspiring place I've been is Bali. It is beautiful, and the people, while desperately poor, have the most positive outlook on life. It puts things into perspective.

Specialty: Handmade Artisan Body Care
214.504.4333, lotussoap.com
Twitter: @lotussoap, facebook.com/lotussoap

Lotus Soap

McKinney, Texas

Handmade. Natural. Unique.

Lotus Soap is a handcrafted bath and body company specializing in handmade coconut milk soap, and offering an array of other skin-loving products including lotion, lip balm, sugar scrub and much more, all created from their own original recipe formulations. Lotus Soap uses only plant-based ingredients and selects each one for the way it will love your skin in the final product.

Photos by Katie Cassidy Photography

Portrait by Kelly Rucker Photography

Luxi

Dallas, Texas

Savvy. Creative. Intelligent.
Luxi is an experiential and lifestyle brand-alliance marketing company. With special emphasis on prestige and luxury brands, Luxi is *the* moxie of original brand marketing events executed with dynamic brand exposure, strategic thought/idea partnering and effective brand collaborations. Having had events featured on national television and print publications, Luxi events draw attention and loyal support. The Luxi experience is peerless and unforgettable. Each event is founded with creative intelligence, market savvy and proprietary panache.

Krista Medlock

Specialties: Brand Marketing and Promotional Events
214.989.3310, 214.516.1709
theluxiexperience.com
krista@theluxiexperience.com
facebook.com/theweekenderdallas
Twitter: @luxiexperience

Q&A

What are your most popular products or services?
Out events: The Brandish, The Weekender, The Uptown Crawl, The Luxi Society and many more to come!

What tip would you give women who are starting a business?
Never question your ability. We business owners possess a special gift: gumption. With that, you have most of what you need. Keep going. Learn and augment your business through challenge.

Who is your role model or mentor?
"It takes a village..." Thank-you to every woman business owner who paved the way. Much of my courage and tenacity is elevated by watching you succeed. And, my mom.

What is your biggest fear?
Not learning to stop enough to enjoy the journey. I don't want to miss one moment of it!

What do you like best about owning a business?
The freedom to make decisions based on my own ethics and values, and the freedom to balance my life the way I choose.

What motivates you on a daily basis?
Honoring my purpose and the opportunity to become a better person and professional every day.

Photos by Matt & Julie Weddings

Lyndsey Jones

Dallas, Texas

Captivating. Entertaining. Sultry.

Lyndsey Jones combines her soothing voice with charming stage presence to create a tranquilizing atmosphere as she performs the best of Alicia Keys, Elton John, Lady Gaga and more. She offers an evening of classic and contemporary arrangements sure to please music aficionados as well as casual listeners. Lyndsey can be found in several locations around Dallas, including Terilli's, The Library Bar and Seasons 52.

Lyndsey Jones

Q&A

What tip would you give women who are starting a business?
Never give up! You may start out small, but if you keep networking and putting yourself out there, you will make it!

What is your motto or theme song?
My motto is "Believe in possibilities." I believe that if you have the heart to do something that you're passionate about, there is nothing stopping you.

What is your biggest fear?
Regret. I want to live life with no regrets, so I try to take up every possible opportunity that comes my way.

Specialty: Vocal/Piano Performance
214.535.8416, lyndseyjones.com
facebook.com/lyndseyjonesmusic
Twitter: @lyndsey_jones

Matt & Julie Weddings

Dallas, Texas

Romantic. Modern. Charming.

Matt & Julie Weddings is a husband-and-wife photography team. Newlyweds themselves, Matt and Julie focus on bright, natural light photography that captures and conveys the raw emotion and joy of people in love.

Specialties: Weddings, Engagements and Bridals
mattandjulieweddings.com
Twitter: @mattjulienorine
Instagram: @julienorine
facebook.com/MattandJulieWeddings

Photos by Matt & Julie Weddings

Q&A

What tip would you give women who are starting a business?
Surround yourself with other entrepreneurs. I am a strong believer in community and have experienced the encouragement that comes from people who are pursuing their dreams just like we are.

Who is your role model or mentor?
My dad. He has never been afraid to chase his dream of owning his own business, and because of that, he's very successful and has a blast doing what he loves.

What place inspires you?
Disneyland. To me the Disney brand is everything romantic, playful and creative. I absolutely love it and the way it speaks to my imagination, and the kid in me.

Photos by Kelly Rucker Photography

The McMillan Firm, P.C.

Preston Center, Dallas

Personalized. Creative. Professional.

The McMillan Firm, P.C., is the perfect firm for individuals and families seeking personalized and quality representation. Focusing on estate planning, probate and corporate matters, Ashley McMillan is committed to treating clients with respect and sensitivity, providing a professional and individual approach to each unique situation. She truly values the trust you place in her firm.

Q&A

What are your most popular products or services?
Wills, trusts, corporate formations and transactions.

What do you like best about owning a business?
Feeling like I have a direct impact on people's lives. Being the person my clients call when they need help.

What motivates you on a daily basis?
Being grateful I get to do what I love. I truly enjoy helping people navigate through legal issues and solving problems. My clients motivate me to be at my best.

Specialties: Pillows, Paintings, Fabric by the Yard
214.793.4113, meganadamsdesigns.com
Twitter: @madamsdesigns
facebook.com/meganadamsdesigns
linkedin.com/in/megan-brooks

Megan Adams Brooks

Q&A

What do you like best about owning a business?
Being able to do what I am passionate about on a day-to-day basis, and the creative freedom it allows for in my work.

What is your biggest fear?
I am not a very fearful person, which I think works to my benefit in my business because it allows me to take risks.

How do you relax?
Going to the lake on weekends with family. Also, reading a good book.

What place inspires you?
Patterns in nature; I recently went to the Virgin Islands and have been very inspired by sea life.

Megan Adams

Dallas, Texas

Distinctive. Evolving. Swanky.

Megan Adams, artist and textile designer, creates original paintings and unique fabric designs. Inspired by patterns and textures in the natural world, first she either draws or paints to come up with the imagery, and then applies her earthy abstractions to a variety of functional items including tech accessories, dinnerware, pillows and fabric by the yard.

Photos by Matt & Julie Weddings

Q&A

What are your most popular products or services?
Our candidates align with our mission: professional women (and men!) who engage in their jobs, focus on getting it done and doing it well and strive for work/life fit.

What place inspires you?
The young women of tomorrow in our schools, colleges and professional organizations provide my inspiration. You need only to watch and listen to know that they have no limits.

How do you relax?
Running, cooking with my children, playing tennis, reading and sharing special moments with friends are my go-tos for relaxing.

Specialties: Search and Staffing for Professionals
214.649.1388, momcorpsdallas.com
facebook.com/momcorpsdallas, Twitter: @momcorpsdallas
linkedin.com/in/cindystrandyared

Mom Corps Dallas

Dallas, Texas

Trusted. Passionate. Engaged.

Mom Corps Dallas is a national search/staffing firm that focuses on the Dallas/Fort Worth market. Through the Mom Corps network, they offer the ability to place candidates through direct owner-candidate relationships in 20 major markets across the United States. With Mom Corps, companies gain a competitive advantage and are able to adapt easily to changing hiring—be it full-time, part-time, permanent, project-based or contract.

Photos by Katie Cassidy Photography

Q&A

What tip would you give women who are starting a business?
Be humble, and appreciate the small accomplishments. Always have small goals to help lead you to the big ones; this will help you stay focused.

Who is your role model or mentor?
Successful entrepreneurs who started with almost nothing. My father who came to America with nothing and accomplished so much. Love you, Dad!

What place inspires you?
People-watching in Los Angeles always inspires my passion for fashion. New York City, for all its amazing storefront windows.

What do you CRAVE?
Time, sleep and a vacation!

Movida Boutique

Uptown, Dallas

Flirty. Trendy. Fun.

Movida Boutique offers contemporary styles that fashion-driven women crave. Movida appeals to women who seek current fashion trends at an affordable price point. Movida always has a fresh array of style choices in order to offer its fashion-savvy customer the opportunity to dress flirty, sexy, glamorous or casual at times.

Specialty: Contemporary Women's Apparel
5321 E Mockingbird Ln, Ste 130, Dallas
214.823.8180, shopmovida.com
facebook.com/MovidaBoutiqueDallas

Photos by Elle Parks Photography

Naila Malik, MD

Dallas, Texas

Dedicated. Compassionate. Comprehensive.

Naila Malik, MD offers comprehensive services and individualized solutions for acne, cosmetic skincare and weight loss. At Naila Malik, MD, what matters most are the results. And if your care isn't as effective as it could be, Dr. Malik will modify your regimen to improve outcome. In short, their professional team strives to give you your best chance for the results that you want.

For all media requests, contact PLAN B PR at alison@planb-pr.com.

Specialties: Acne & Cosmetic Skincare, Medical Weight Loss
888.210.9693, nailamalikmdskin.com
Twitter: @nailamd

Naila Malik, MD

Q&A

What are your most popular products or services?

Medical weight loss, liquid face-lift and CO^2 fractional laser resurfacing. Our acne skincare products and treatments are unconventional and have led to better-than-average results for most patients.

What tip would you give women who are starting a business?

Persistence and perseverance are the keys to success. If you make up your mind to achieve something meaningful, don't let anyone or anything stop you.

What do you CRAVE?

Success, in achieving both personal and professional goals, which is a moving target. I consider myself a student of life and strive to be a better individual every day.

Nan Lee Jewelry

McKinney, Texas

Inspiring. Meaningful. Timeless.

Step inside Nan Lee's stunning boutique, and you are instantly captivated by delicate and timeless jewelry created in-house and by artists from around the world. The perfect destination for the perfect gift, Nan Lee Jewelry has something beautiful for everyone.

Specialty: Jewelry
106 W Virginia St, McKinney, 972.540.2739
nanleejewelry.com, Twitter: @nanleejewelry
facebook.com/nanleejewelry

Photos by Elle Parks Photography

Q&A

What is your motto or theme song?
Live a balanced life: learn some and think some and draw and paint and sing and dance and play and work every day some.

What tip would you give women who are starting a business?
Write down your vision and plan. When obstacles come up or when you're feeling distracted, go back to your vision statement and stick to it!

What motivates you on a daily basis?
My wonderful customers. Knowing that my jewelry is a part of someone's special occasion or milestone makes me strive for excellence in every part of my business.

Natalie Pitts Photography

Dallas, Texas

Modern. Real. Visionary.

Natalie Pitts is a professional photographer in the Dallas–Fort Worth area specializing in portrait and wedding photography. She has a simplistic style, while also adding a touch of originality and creativity to every image. Capturing the realness and true personalities of her subjects is what she loves the most. Natalie Pitts Photography provides clients with quality images that they can enjoy for a lifetime.

Specialty: Photography
972.342.9529
blog.nataliepittsphotography.com
Twitter: @NataliePPhoto

Photos by Natalie Pitts

Q&A

What tip would you give women who are starting a business?
Participate in networking events and get to know people in your industry. My business wouldn't be where it is now if it wasn't for the friendships I've made through networking!

What is your biggest fear?
I've always been afraid of driving behind car carriers on the highways because one of the cars might not be attached correctly and fall off right in front of me!

What do you CRAVE?
Traveling! Traveling! Traveling! I love visiting new places and experiencing other cultures!

New Friends New Life

Dallas, Texas

Encouraging. Empowering. Effective.

Abused, abandoned and exploited... until finding New Friends New Life. NFNL offers holistic, transformational healing from domestic sex exploitation. Sex trafficking preys on the most vulnerable—young girls—abused in childhood, thrown away as teens and exploited as women. Join the Circle of Friends, a group of volunteers helping with clients or with special events such as the WINGS Luncheon, Golf Classic or Home Tour.

Specialties: Transforming Women's and Children's Lives
214.965.0935, newfriendsnewlife.org
Twitter: @nfnlnews, facebook.com/newfriendsnewlife
linkedin.com/in/newfriendsnewlife

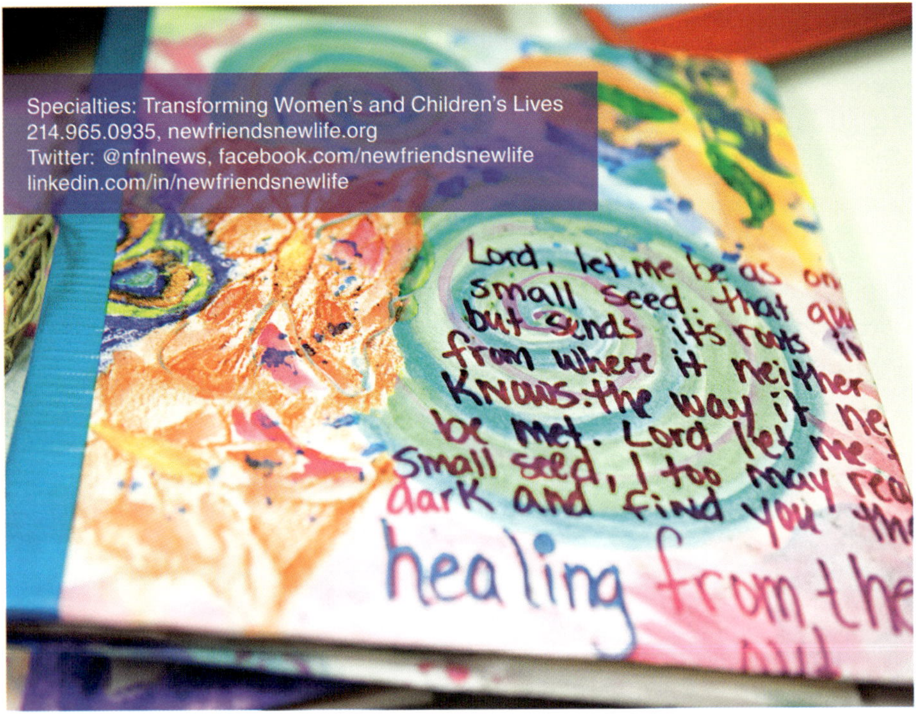

Photos by Elle Parks Photography

Katie Pedigo

Q&A

What are your most popular products or services?

Rescuing and restoring the lives of victims of domestic sexual exploitation and trafficking. NFNL helps women overcome abuse, addiction and poverty by providing education, job training, mental health and spiritual support.

What tip would you give women who are starting a business?

Join the movement to end sexual exploitation. NFNL partners with local businesses to offer employment opportunities. You can help by offering permanent placements, temporary assignments and internships.

Photos by Elle Parks Photography

Nine-Eighteen

Turtle Creek, Dallas

Timeless. Artistic. Distinctive.

Nine-Eighteen is Dallas's newest boutique jewelry experience. Located on Turtle Creek, Nine-Eighteen offers customers a comfortable, intimate setting for a memorable shopping experience. It's not about the next commission or the ten other shoppers hanging around; it's all about you. And then, there are the jewels... Nine-Eighteen offers distinctive, eye-catching jewels for every price range: from classic, understated pieces to the over-the-top bling-tastic.

Q&A

What are your most popular products or services?

Nine-Eighteen specializes in engagement rings, wedding bands, celebration rings and fashion jewelry for both men and women from a group of fresh, innovative designers and our own custom creations.

What do you like best about owning a business?

I like knowing that I'm responsible for my successes and failures. I'm not waiting on someone else to validate my worth.

What do you CRAVE?

Freedom: the freedom to choose to do what I want to do, to have the family I've always wanted and to marry the man of my dreams!

Q&A

Who is your role model or mentor?
My mother for teaching me grace and compassion while instilling a fierce work ethic in all that I do! My husband for his love, support, guidance and reality checks: all are invaluable.

What is your motto or theme song?
Two people in my career have said phrases that have stuck: "Slow and steady win the race," and "you are either making me money or costing me money."

What do you CRAVE?
More time to love and accomplish what God's will is for my life. Leaving a legacy that's not related to work.

Noble Grace, LLC

Dallas, Texas

Experienced. Passionate. Effective.

Noble Grace is an energy-consulting firm that works with oil and gas companies in the area of regulatory compliance. Noble Grace specializes in Department of Transportation regulations, and their services are designed to satisfy the needs of a dynamic energy industry in the midst of today's challenging business and regulatory environments.

Specialties: Regulatory Compliance and Consulting for Oil and Gas Companies
817.419.0001, noblegrace.co, Twitter: @dsbelltexas
facebook.com/NobleGraceLLC

Photos by Matt & Julie Weddings

Photo by Matt & Julie Weddings

"Stay true to yourself... always. Don't compare yourself! It's not the end of the world if you make a mistake. Don't take every opportunity that comes your way. Breathe and pray."

—Darla S. Bell of Noble Grace, LLC

Occhiali Modern Optics

University Park, Texas

Distinctive. Sophisticated. Current.

Occhiali Modern Optics helps clients find the perfect luxury eyewear for their faces, personalities and lifestyles. Their staff is made up of trained opticians who are fashion-savvy and informed. Occhiali Modern Optics strives to help you project your image with the perfect eyewear.

Photos by Matt & Julie Weddings

Specialty: High-end Fashion Eyewear
8300 Preston Road, Ste 310, University Park, 214.368.2777
occhialimodernoptics.com, facebook.com/occhialimodernoptics

Lisa Methvin, owner, with Sara McDaniel, ABOC, manager

Q&A

What are your most popular products or services?
Handmade, high-quality eyewear. We pride ourselves in creating a memorable eyewear-fitting experience, filling complex prescriptions and presenting an unmatched eyewear showroom.

What tip would you give women who are starting a business?
Allow your vision and your inspiration to bring your business decisions into focus.

What place inspires you?
Yellowstone National Park. With its massive grandeur, it humbles all with its beauty.

What do you CRAVE?
Time. Does anyone have enough?

Photo by Matt & Julie Weddings

"Our motto is 'learn from the past, live in the moment, create your own destiny.'"

—Lisa Methvin and Sara McDaniel of Occhiali Modern Optics

Q&A

What are your most popular products or services?
Our WordPress sites are by far the most popular. WordPress is currently the #1 content management system worldwide, powering more than 73 million websites!

What tip would you give women who are starting a business?
Seek out and maintain a network of professional contacts. Not only will they provide you with valuable advice for your business, but they will also be a source for your clients.

Who is your role model or mentor?
My father. Over the years I have watched him start up and grow several successful companies. I learned so much, but admit I still keep him on speed dial.

Old Kinderhook Productions

Dallas, Texas

Interactive. Organized. Timely.

Old Kinderhook Productions designs websites and online tools to empower businesses to connect with the 21st-century consumer. Old Kinderhook uses a clearly scheduled, approachable process to guide clients from the "I need a website!" phase through the launch of a custom, completed site.

Specialties: HTML, WordPress and E-Commerce Websites
469.964.9382, oldkinderhook.net
Twitter: @L_M_Henry, linkedin.com/in/laurenmhenry

Photos by Kelly Rucker Photography

Park Cities Dance

Park Cities, Dallas

Expressive. Fun. Contemporary.
Park Cities Dance is DFW's first metropolitan dance and theater studio complex, where students aged 18 months to adults enjoy top arts instruction in airy world-class facilities. Patterned on the great schools in New York and London, with classes ranging from ballet to film acting to opera, more than 700 Dallas children and adults elect to study only or study and perform, no matter their age and ability.

Specialties: Dance, Singing, Acting and Dance Fitness
7979 Inwood Rd, Stes 101 and 201, Dallas, 213.357.8888
parkcitiesdance.com, Twitter: @ParkCitiesDance
facebook.com/parkcitiesdance, linkedin.com/in/jacquelineporter

Upper left photo by Jacqueline Porter, upper middle photo by Blair Chambers, lower left and upper right photos by Tracee Bennett, portrait by Miranda Pereyda

Q&A

What are your most popular products or services?
Award-winning classical ballet for students aged 18 months to adults (beginner to professional) is #1, with musical theater, hip-hop, acro, singing, parties, wedding dances, party entertainment and flash mobs at #2!

What motivates you on a daily basis?
I've always had an inner fire. But when I started this business (knowing not one person in Dallas), belief that I could offer something wonderful sustained me through the difficulties.

What is your motto or theme song?
The Laverne and Shirley theme song! Nothin's gonna turn us back now, Straight ahead and on the track now. We're gonna make our dreams come true, Doin' it our way!

Photos by Katie Cassidy Photography

Penny Crosson

Dallas, Texas

Engaging. Professional. Empowering.

Penny is creative, captivating and a breath of fresh air in the beauty industry. She brings over 25 years of professional services and regimens to this exciting ever-changing industry. She has a graceful approach with realistic methods and cost-saving solutions that bring empowerment to anyone. Looking and feeling your best is essential to succeeding in every area of your life.

Q&A

What tip would you give women who are starting a business?
Know your market and understand your customer. Find a unique niche. Stay true to yourself and do not lose sight of your purpose.

What do you like best about owning a business?
I love knowing that my business is built on my integrity and the things which I am truly passionate about.

What inspires you?
I love to empower others by helping them find ways to enhance beauty and energy in their life. It is empowering to lead people to solutions for their individuality.

Lacy and Julie Thomas

Q&A

What tip would you give women who are starting a business?
You must put your business first. If you can't be there for your business, then you can't expect it to be there for you.

Who is your role model or mentor?
Our parents. They have always taught us to believe in ourselves, and they gave us the confidence to do anything in life.

How do you relax?
Lacy: I like to cook with a glass of wine by my side and Fleetwood Mac playing in the background.
Julie: Sitting on my balcony with a glass of wine.

What place inspires you?
Home: where we relax, recharge and discover new ideas to grow our business.

Pieces

Highland Park, Dallas

Eclectic. Affordable. Classic.
Pieces is a contemporary women's clothing boutique located in Snider Plaza. The owners are two close-knit sisters from Houston who graduated from Louisiana State University. They aim to bring a mix of Southern charm and big city into their store with fashion-forward styles and wallet-friendly prices for all age groups.

Specialty: One-stop Shopping
6723 Snider Plaza, Dallas, 214.265.7802
piecesclothingboutique.com, Twitter: @Piecesclothing
facebook.com/piecesclothingboutique

Photos by Matt & Julie Weddings

Q&A

What are your most popular products or services?
Private one-on-one sessions are still the most popular due to the individual attention for the client. Reformer and Redcord classes are the most popular classes.

What do you like best about owning a business?
Realizing there was a need and watching my vision come to life. It's very rewarding to see the benefits and impact it has on people's lives.

What motivates you on a daily basis?
My clients. The best part of this business are the people. Working with different bodies, assisting each one in meeting their specific goals and seeing the rewards they get.

Pilates Connection

Park Cities, Dallas

Inspiring. Personal. Healing.

Pilates Connection is more than a Pilates studio, it's a therapeutic experience. From the spa-like environment to the highly skilled and medically knowledgeable instructors, clients are rewarded with an overall body and mind transformation. Providing the classical system of Pilates along with the new and innovative Redcord functional training system, Pilates Connection offers clients the most effective and efficient method in achieving overall health.

Specialty: Pilates
By appointment: 6043 Sherry Ln, Dallas, 214.668.6469
pilatesconnection.co, Twitter: @pilates_CX
facebook.com/PilatesConnection

Photos by Natalie Pitts

PLAN B PR

Dallas, Texas

Committed. Loyal. Passionate.
As a boutique public relations firm, PLAN B PR services a roster of clients that exist at the intersection of sports, food, design, philanthropy, hospitality, entertainment and fashion. With an emphasis on PR, events and other non-traditional marketing, PLAN B PR is dedicated to growing the company brand. From grand openings to branding, marketing and public relations, they target all aspects of the industry in order to achieve their clients' goals. Photos shown are examples of the exemplary work PLAN B PR executes.

Specialty: Public Relations
By appointment: 3625 N Hall St, Ste 530, Dallas
214.577.2965, planb-pr.com, Twitter: @planbpr
facebook.com/PLANBPublicRelations, linkedin.com/in/bricrum

Photos on opposite page by Shana Anderson

Bri Crum

Q&A

What tip would you give women who are starting a business?
Be confident and focused. Work hard, and don't pass up any opportunity. Be true to yourself and follow your heart. Keep it simple!

What do you like best about owning a business?
Having the freedom to make my own decisions that are best for our clients and partners. It feels amazing to give my team an opportunity to have a successful career.

How do you relax?
Having cocktails with friends, going to my mom's house on the lake and decorating my house. And getting out of Dallas to travel!

Photo by Shana Anderson

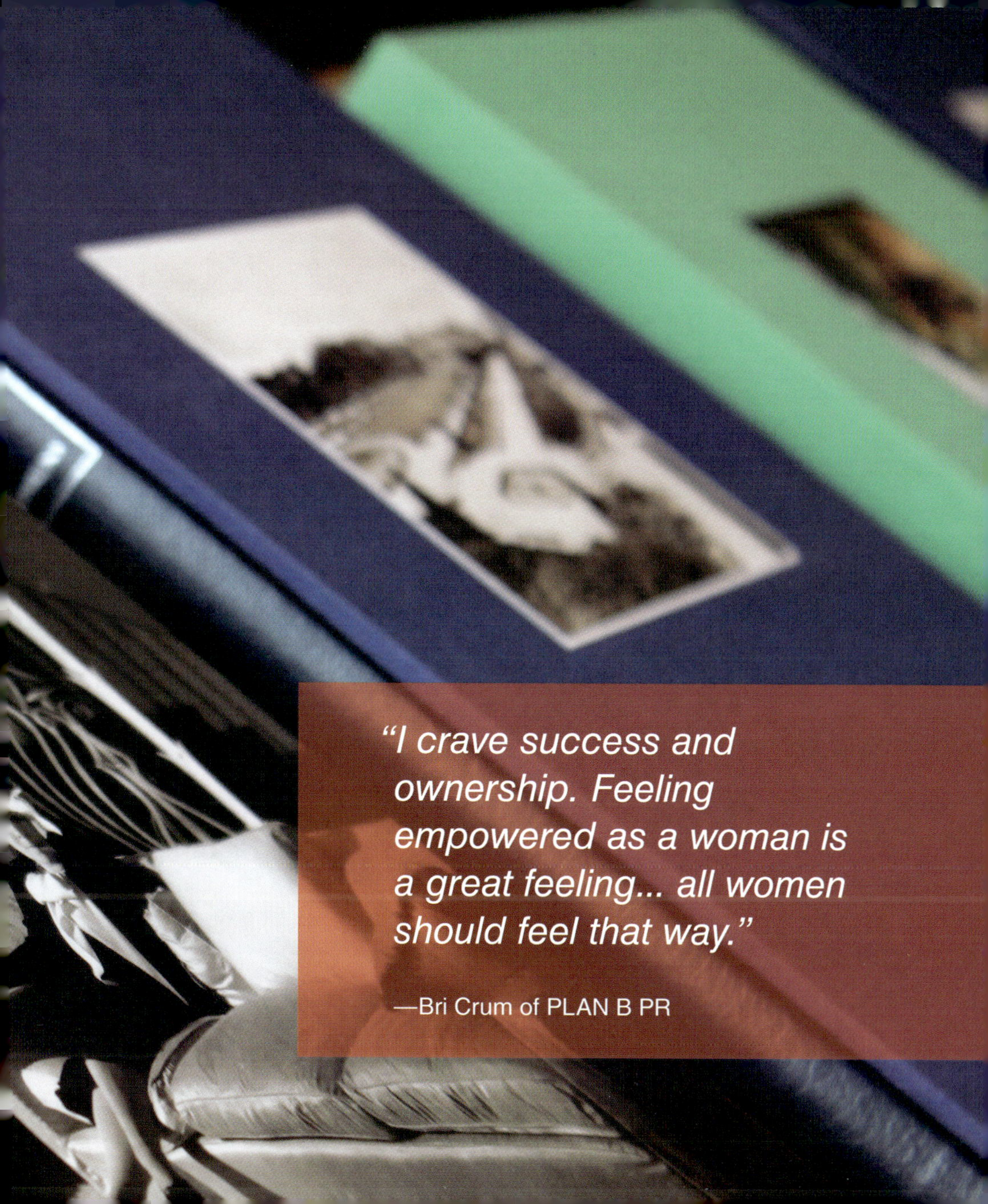

"I crave success and ownership. Feeling empowered as a woman is a great feeling... all women should feel that way."

—Bri Crum of PLAN B PR

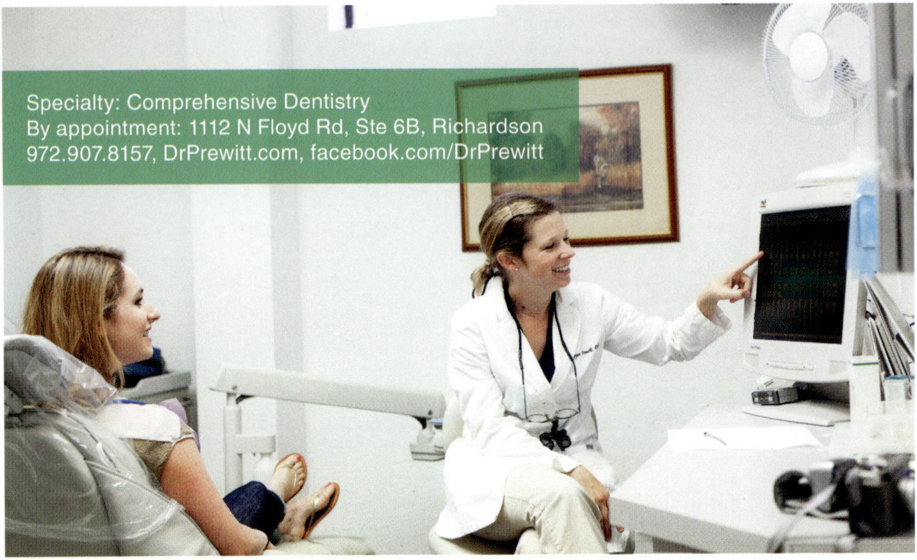

Specialty: Comprehensive Dentistry
By appointment: 1112 N Floyd Rd, Ste 6B, Richardson
972.907.8157, DrPrewitt.com, facebook.com/DrPrewitt

Photos by Natalie Pitts

Prewitt Family Dentistry

Richardson, Texas

Friendly. Ethical. Thorough.
Prewitt Family Dentistry is a place where all basic dental needs can be met for all ages, especially kids! Dr. Prewitt is a third-generation dentist who's passion is creating an atmosphere of trust and comfort with her patients. Her staff accommodates Spanish, Hebrew and Russian speakers, too!

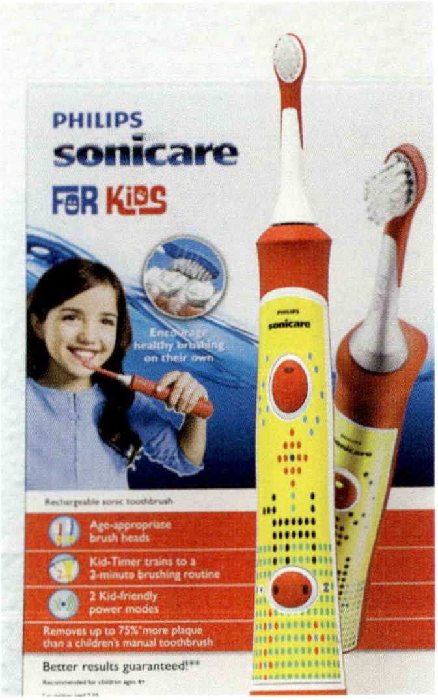

Regan Prewitt

Q&A

What tip would you give women who are starting a business?
Do whatever you can to incorporate your personality. Don't try to be someone you're not because authenticity is contagious and attractive.

What motivates you on a daily basis?
I am energized by the diversity of personalities I get to see each day, and love the opportunity to connect and learn from so many different people.

How do you relax?
I love to cook and try new recipes! The food network has changed my life.

What place inspires you?
The Dallas Arboretum because it's a place where I can relax, be surrounded by beauty and remember it's not all about me.

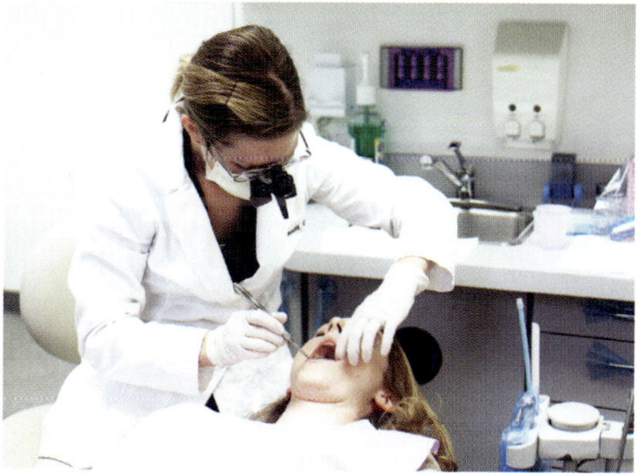

Jeny Honea

Q&A

What do you like best about owning a business?
The joy that comes from making people happy!

How do you relax?
In a quiet rural place, simply meditating on the beauty of nature, on the beach with a book listening to the waves crash, gardening or crafting.

What do you CRAVE?
Time with my kids, good health, peace, love and laughter.

What tip would you give women who are starting a business?
Go with your first instinct, and always believe in yourself!

Primp

Salon*Boutique*Garden

McKinney, Texas

Stylish. Unique. Creative.

Primp is focused on your every need. Whether you are in need of a new hairstyle or wardrobe, a relaxing hand or foot treatment or are simply searching for the perfect gift, let the Primp staff "primp" your life gorgeous! Their house-made, all-natural scrubs and lotions are available for purchase in the boutique. Also, take your pick of the unique and beautiful, repurposed planters on display throughout the store.

Specialties: Natural Nail Care, Hair, Gifts, Unique Planters
Boutique & Garden: 114 S Tennessee St, McKinney, 972.542.2775
Salon & Spa: 116 S Tennessee St, McKinney, 972.542.2775
primpsalonboutique.com, facebook.com/primpsalonboutique

Photos by Elle Parks Photography

Q&A

What motivates you on a daily basis?
Pride.

How do you relax?
Would you believe flea markets? Especially with India, my 16-year-old daughter. We love to hunt and gather, and she has a keen sense when it comes to picking.

What place inspires you?
Other people's homes. I am so intrigued by other peoples' style, and how they showcase their family treasures.

What do you like best about owning a business?
When a customer "gets it," understands our concept and appreciates our efforts and services.

Random

Lakewood, Dallas

Unexpected. Quirky. Fun.

Random is a treasure chest of a shop that holds a plethora of distinctive and unusual objects to add oomph to your home or to bestow upon your best friend. Complimentary gift wrap is always finished off with a hand-tied bow. The family-owned business is proud to offer handmade goods from local artists and will always pick "Made in the USA" over imported merchandise.

Specialties: Unique Home Accessories and Gifts
Hillside Village Shopping Center, 6465 E Mockingbird Lane, Ste 366, Dallas
214.827.9499, shopatrandom.com, facebook.com/ShopAtRandom
Twitter: @shop_at_random

Photos by Matt & Julie Weddings

Ruthie's Rolling Cafe

Dallas, Texas

Tasty. Fun. Nostalgic.

Ruthie's Rolling Cafe is a grilled cheese food truck offering the best melt-in-your-mouth grilled cheese sandwiches to the DFW area. It's a fact that everyone loves a great grilled cheese sandwich; the ultimate American comfort food! Ruthie's takes Grandmother's nostalgic cheesy recipes and prepares them with love in a "kitchen on wheels."

Specialty: Gourmet Grilled Cheese Sandwiches
ruthiesrollingcafe.com, Twitter: @ruthiesrolling
facebook.com/ruthiesrollingcafe

Photos by Matt & Julie Weddings

Q&A

What are your most popular products or services?
Our grilled cheese sandwiches are amazing. You can't beat our Patty Melt with grilled onions on sourdough or our chicken, mozzarella and pesto—yum!

What tip would you give women who are starting a business?
Set realistic, attainable goals and stay the course.

What do you like best about owning a business?
Every day is a new adventure.

What do you CRAVE?
Crepes! By the way, our crepe truck is coming soon!

Melanie Borges and Monica Whitaker

Q&A

What tip would you give women who are starting a business?
Make sure you have a great support team and talents of all kinds so that you can create a successful business.

What do you like best about owning a business?
We love being in control of our own success and having the freedom to surround ourselves with a positive environment.

Who is your role model or mentor?
Our mother has always been our role model. She has overcome tremendous obstacles to support us and make us the women we are today.

Say it with Sugar Cake Shop

Wylie, Texas

Hip. Scrumptious. Artistic.

Say it with Sugar is your one-stop shop for all your sugar needs, from desserts to whimsical cakes. All of their creations are handmade on-site with the finest ingredients to maintain the freshest products. Cakes are all custom-created for your special events. Say it with Sugar is located in historic downtown Wylie, so come down, check them out and pick up some goodies to go.

Specialties: Baked Goods, Custom Order Cakes, Cupcakes, Chocolates
106 N Ballard Ave, Wylie, 972.442.3613
sayitwithsugar.com, facebook.com/sayitwithsugar

Photos by Natalie Pitts

She Reigns

Dallas, Texas

Fashionable. Functional. Chic.

She Reigns makes fashion-forward outerwear that will keep you dry and fabulous as you embark on all your journeys—great and small. She Reigns creates jackets that are as functional as they are fabulous. Based in Dallas and made in the USA.

Specialty: Fashion-forward Rainwear
shereigns.com, Twitter: @Shereignsstyle
facebook.com/SheReignsStyle

Photos by Blake Towsley, except portrait by Matt & Julie Weddings

Cathy and Jenica Williamson

Q&A

What tip would you give women who are starting a business?
It comes with challenges and bumps in the road, but take it one day at a time and you will figure it all out.

What do you like best about owning a business?
We love the challenge of offering such a special product. We want our name to become synonymous with fashionable rainwear and help you look chic while you stay dry.

What place inspires you?
Home, because it's the place where we can totally be ourselves.

SitterCentralDallas

Dallas, Texas

Innovative. Reliable. Creative.

SitterCentralDallas is an online service that simplifies busy life by providing reliable, trustworthy sitters and nannies in Dallas. SitterCentralDallas takes the worry out of finding the perfect candidate because each one is personally interviewed, CPR-certified, and background- and reference-checked. SitterCentralDallas is the worry-free way to keep a household running smoothly. They provide full-time, part-time or help when in a bind.

Specialty: Childcare Services
214.697.5846, sittercentraldallas.com
facebook.com/SitterCentralDallas, Twitter: @sittercentral
linkedin.com/in/rlogan317

Photos by Catie Ronquillo

Q&A

What are your most popular products or services?
Placing babysitters, semi-permanent and permanent nannies into busy households.

What tip would you give women who are starting a business?
Determination is key: creating a business may take longer than expected. Your business model must be solid enough so that word-of-mouth referrals can drive the business to a successful level.

What do you like best about owning a business?
There are no limitations to creativity, to levels of success or the amount of earning potential. You also have the ability to contribute and leave a positive mark on society.

Social Shots Photo Booth

McKinney, Texas

Entertaining. Memorable. Nostalgic.
Social Shots offers unique photo and video booth rentals for weddings, holiday parties, birthdays and corporate events. A modern design paired with the old-school charm of a traditional photo booth embedded with the latest technology enables guests to enjoy unlimited photos, HD video messaging, silly props, the fun of building a one-of-a-kind guestbook and DVD as a lasting keepsake.

Specialty: Photo/Video Booth Rentals
865.272.9249, socialshotsphoto.com
facebook.com/socialshots, Twitter: @socialshots

Photos by Catie Ronquillo

Q&A

What tip would you give women who are starting a business?
Find a mentor early on who will guide you and support you along the way, and if you make a mistake, learn from it and be better because of it.

What is your biggest fear?
Not following my dreams out of fear of failure. Life has so many amazing things to offer, and I want to experience as much of it as possible.

What place inspires you?
Nature, it brings me back to my childhood and reminds me of all God's beautiful creation. The peace of the quietness refreshes my soul and is very inspiring.

Photos by Apryl Ann Photography, except lower right photo (opposite page) by Sarah Kate, Photographer

Southern Fried Paper

Dallas, Texas

Artistic. Elegant. Luxurious.

Southern Fried Paper specializes in custom invitations and event branding for high-class affairs. Everything from paper selection to the printing process is tailored to each unique event. Every design is truly one-of-a-kind, and the creative team takes pride in attention to detail. The studio's innovative stationery has been featured around the world in publications such as *Martha Stewart Weddings*, *Southern Living Weddings* and *Brides Magazine* (UK).

Chelsea Carpenter

Q&A

What are your most popular products or services?
Custom wedding invitations and corporate event branding. Our clients want a design that no one else will have. We also create coordinating event decor like menus and signage.

What motivates you on a daily basis?
I love seeing designs go from preliminary concepts to beautiful finished products that make an event unforgettable.

What do you like best about owning a business?
The fabulous people I get to work with. I have met so many ambitious women driven by their enthusiasm and love of their craft.

Specialties: Event Branding, Custom Design, Invitations
214.919.0731
SouthernFriedPaper.com
facebook.com/SouthernFriedPaper
Twitter: @SFPdallas

Photo by n.Barrett Photography

"You must love what you do. If you're passionate about it, then the late nights and hard work will pay off."

—Chelsea Carpenter of Southern Fried Paper

Fatesta Bateman

Q&A

What tip would you give women who are starting a business?
Price your products and services based on the value you bring to each customer. Don't underestimate your worth.

What do you like best about owning a business?
I like knowing that every day I'm working toward my dream and my purpose in life.

What is your motto or theme song?
My motto is: No weeds, just seeds.

What place inspires you and why?
I'm inspired by Barnes and Nobles. I love being around so much information and the great smell of coffee. It's a great concept, and I love it.

The Spa Bar

Design District, Dallas

Versatile. Intimate. Contemporary.
Located in the Design District, The Spa Bar is a uniquely designed destination for private parties and VIP event services.

Specialties: Private Parties and VIP Event Services
1308 Conant St, Dallas, 214.716.0529, thespabar.com
facebook.com/TheSpaBar, Twitter: @thespabar

Photos by Catie Ronquillo and Monica Salazar Photography

Q&A

What motivates you on a daily basis?
Knowing that my work helps to inspire young children and their families to want to read. It opens up great possibilities for children of all different backgrounds and learning styles.

What is your motto or theme song?
Storyopolis Entertainment is where "Art Inspires Reading." When a child's mind is peaked with curiosity and delight over great art, the desire to read the words on the page blossoms.

What place inspires you and why?
The library. It can be the most magical and imaginative place on the planet that also builds your potential to succeed in school and life.

Storyopolis Entertainment

Dallas, Texas

Unique. Community-minded. Respected.

Storyopolis Entertainment is an unrivaled showcase for contemporary art and illustrations from children's picture books. It offers a uniquely reliable and reputable meeting place where the finest talents in the world of children's books can connect with the virtuosos of the media/entertainment industry. Storyopolis Entertainment is a platform to promote literacy. It sponsors an Author/Illustrator Speaker Series and brings great literary celebrities to schools and libraries.

Specialties: Original Illustrations from Children's Picture Books and Contemporary Art
214.796.6556, 818.441.2347
storyopolisentertainment.com, storyopolisart.com

Photos by Claire McCormack

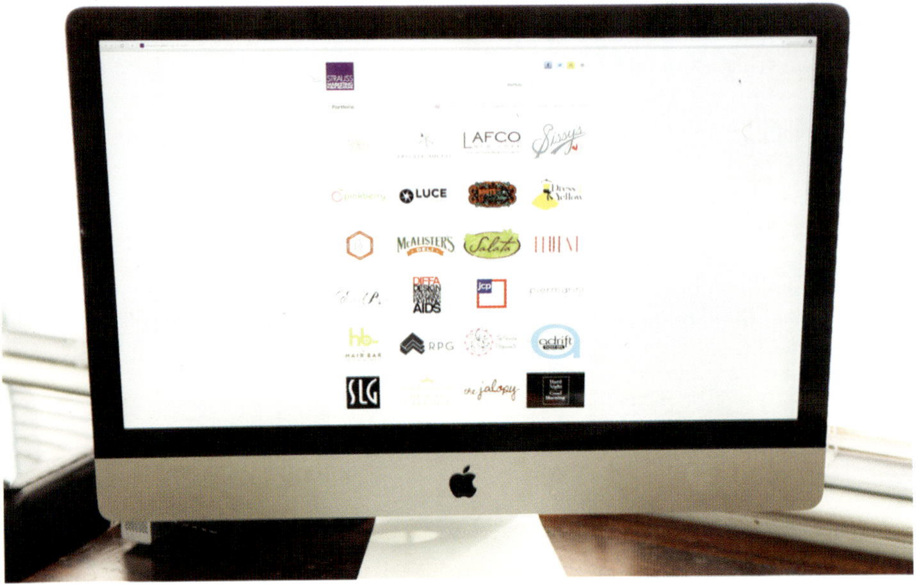

Left photo by Claire McCormack, portrait by Elizabeth Lippman, lower right photo by Kristina Bowman

Strauss Marketing Public Relations

Dallas, Texas

Dedicated. Unique. Inventive.

After many successful years as a project manager with a real estate group in Dallas, Jenifer branched out to start her own company, Strauss Marketing Public Relations, in 2001. Four years later, she expanded the company to NYC. Since then, the company has grown to represent clients in a range of industries including culinary, beauty, retail, fashion and business development in Texas, New York and beyond.

Jenifer Strauss Dannhauser

Q&A

What are your most popular products or services?
Introducing and keeping brands relevant to consumers via strategic initiatives.

What tip would you give women who are starting a business?
Figure out what it is you love to do because owning a business becomes more than just a job—it's your life.

What do you like best about owning a business?
Being able to do what I love every day, surrounded by people I care about.

What motivates you on a daily basis?
At first, it was learning as much as possible to achieve goals I set for myself. At this point in my career, it's sharing what I've learned with my team.

Specialties: Marketing and Public Relations, Brand Development
214.352.6700, straussmarketing-pr.com
facebook.com/jeniferastrauss, Twitter: @jeniferastrauss

Studio Ten 25

Dallas, Texas

Approachable. Stunning. Livable.

Studio Ten 25 was founded by interior designer Abbe Fenimore in 2007. Abbe's experience began by representing interior finish products and has flourished from there, encompassing everything from furniture design to commercial and residential interiors. Abbe's style is an eclectic balance of vibrant color, a mix of rich materials and a true sense of space.

Shop Ten 25

Dallas, Texas

Colorful. Chic. Well-edited.

Shop Ten 25 is a collection of well-edited, high-style pieces curated by Abbe. The exclusively online store ranges in style from glamour to rustic and from furniture to lighting and accessories. Thanks to Abbe's keen eye, rare and hard-to-find designer style is right at your fingertips with a moderate price tag.

Photos by Melanie Johnson, except portrait by Bret Sano

Specialty: Interior Design

Studio Ten 25: 214.763.3040, studioten25.com
Twitter: @studioten25, facebook.com/studioten25

Shop Ten 25: 214.763.3040, shopten25.com
Twitter: @shopten25, facebook.com/ShopTen25

linkedin.com/in/studioten25

Abbe Fenimore

Q&A

What tip would you give women who are starting a business?
Have a plan, and be prepared for it to change as your business grows! Having a direction for your business is a must, but being flexible will make you better.

What motivates you on a daily basis?
As cliché as the motivational sayings are, they really do work! I have a few in my office to remind me to keep going when I am ready to quit.

What place inspires you?
I love browsing through beautifully curated shops. Ceylon et Cie is one of my favorite places. I could spend hours taking in the unique pieces from around the world.

"All fear stands for is 'false evidence appearing real.' I constantly remind myself of the wonderful experiences I have had by facing my fears."

—Abbe Fenimore of Studio Ten 25 and Shop Ten 25

Photo by Melanie Johnson

Amanda Embry

Q&A

What are your most popular products or services?
Haircuts and color, hair extensions, Brazilian blowouts, massage therapy, nails, skincare, eyelash extensions, makeup, waxing and photography.

What place inspires you?
California's laid-back bohemian look. Off-the-shoulder tops, long hippie skirts and vintage jewelry are all things you will find here.

What tip would you give women who are starting a business?
Learn time management and put it to good use. Someone will always need you for something, so make sure you have designated "office hours" that are off-limits.

The Style House

Frisco, Texas

Hip. Trendy. Fun.

The Style House is a place that incorporates “all things style” from salon services to photography and even a boutique where one can find jewelry, designer apparel and more. The Style House features the industry’s top professionals in hair color and cuts, blowouts and extensions, massage therapy, skincare, nailcare, makeup and eyelash extensions. And they serve homemade bread daily on their coffee bar!

Specialties: Salon and Spa Services, Designer Apparel
7127 Main St, Frisco, 469.287.2823
stylehousefrisco.com, Twitter: @7127main

Photos by Katie Cassidy Photography

Q&A

What tip would you give women who are starting a business?
Jump right in. Your passion will carry you through trials and learning what you don't yet know.

Who is your role model or mentor?
My mom has always been my role model. Her ability to become a published writer inspires me and shows me what an independent woman can accomplish.

What place inspires you?
Any cluttered area—I see the potential hiding underneath.

What do you CRAVE?
A trip to my birthplace, Morocco!

Styled & Organized Living

Dallas, Texas

Organized. Efficient. Creative.

Styled & Organized Living organizes your living space and offers practical ideas for your home, image consulting and home staging. Leticia enjoys helping people take back their space while fine-tuning their image, all while utilizing stylish solutions because "Life is Better Organized"!

Photos by Catie Ronquillo

Susan Posnick

Q&A

What tip would you give women who are starting a business?
You can't be good at everything, so find people to work with who are experts in their area and let them do their job. And be prepared to make mistakes.

What do you CRAVE?
Continued growth personally and in my business, more quiet breaths, designer vintage everything and red-soled shoes.

What do you like best about owning a business?
The greatest joy comes from cultivating business and personal relationships, and knowing the satisfaction of developing unique products that simplify women's beauty routines while protecting their skin from sun damage.

Susan Posnick Cosmetics

Dallas, Texas

Easy. Travel-friendly. Healthy.
Susan's background as a celebrity makeup artist and skin cancer survivor inspired her to create a cosmetics line for real women in real life. Her products are fun to use and multipurpose, and they'll go through security in their own mesh bag or they can be tossed into a tennis bag. Sold the world over in prestigious spas, apothecaries, specialty retail stores, medical offices and airports, Susan Posnick makes you look better—naturally!

Portrait and upper left photo by Claire McCormack

Specialties: Color Cosmetics and Natural Sun Protection
214.747.2111, susanposnick.com
Twitter: @SusanPosnick, linkedin.com/in/susan-posnick

Photos by Katie Cassidy Photography

Sweet Bee Candy Emporium

Dallas, Texas

Unique. Meaningful. Inspiring.
Be sweet—everybody loves candy! From bulk candy to beautifully packaged gifts, Sweet Bee Candy Emporium is your one-stop shop for everything candy. Sweet Bee offers a variety of ways to add some sugar to your life. With over 100 different types of candy, sourced across the globe, Sweet Bee has a treat for every occasion.

Christie Kimbell and Deb Corley

Q&A

What tip would you give women who are starting a business?

Don't overthink it—take the first step. Surround yourself with people who inspire you. Find something you love—you need the passion to keep the perseverance.

What are your most popular products or services?

Sweet Bee Candy Emporium offers a candy for every occasion. Our most popular products are our bulk items, branded candy, personalized favors and SweetCards.

What do you like best about owning a business?

The opportunity to build an experience and create products that truly make people happy.

Specialties: Sweet Candy, SweetCards, Bulk Candy and Favors
214.347.9006, sweetbeeemporium.com
Twitter: @SweetBeeCandy

Photo by Katie Cassidy Photography

"We CRAVE those moments with friends and family when you feel a sense of peace and just know that everything is right with the world!"

—Christie Kimbell and Deb Corley of Sweet Bee Candy Emporium

Angie Conard and Patti Otte

Q&A

What are your most popular products or services?
Customers love our unique flavors, such as Sea Salt Caramel, Bourbon Vanilla and Kooky Monster. SnoBalls—a combination of ice cream and shaved ice—are also hugely popular.

What motivates you on a daily basis?
The smiles on our littlest customers' faces! Looking out over a packed house and witnessing customers making connections, having fun, creating community. Watching life and love happen before our eyes.

What is your motto or theme song?
"The time to be happy is now.
The place to be happy is here.
The way to be happy is to make others so." —Robert Ingersoll

Specialties: Handmade Ice Cream, Shaved Ice, Toffee, Candies
2701 Custer Parkway, Ste 810, Richardson, 972.635.5635
sweetfirefly.com, facebook.com/sweetfireflyrichardson

Sweet Firefly

Gourmet Ice Cream and Candied Treats

Richardson, Texas

Inviting. Inspired. Unique.

Sweet Firefly showcases a unique variety of handmade ice creams and an array of delectable candies. Nestled in the heart of Richardson's Canyon Creek neighborhood, this sweet shop also serves coffee, shaved ice year-round and other seasonal goodies. Sweet Firefly offers guests both simple goodness and a warm, welcoming environment.

Photos by Katie Cassidy Photography

Tannery & Company Wealth Management

Richardson, Texas

Passionate. Individualized. Independent.

Tannery & Company Wealth Management creates solutions designed to help clients live without financial worry or regret. Working in a true partnership, the firm informs and educates clients to make decisions to enhance their life. Relationships are personal, professional and based on passionate, individualized business approaches that translate client concerns, desires and goals into enriching life plans. Securities are offered through LPL Financial, Member FINRA/SIPC.

Specialty: Financial Guidance
2701 Custer Parkway, Ste 819, Richardson
214.239.4700, tannerywealth.com
facebook.com/tannerywealth
linkedin.com/in/TinaTannery

Photos by Kelly Rucker Photography

Q&A

What are your most popular products or services?

Our planning service—not having a plan is like taking a road trip without a map or GPS. Your plan becomes the blueprint for your success.

What tip would you give women who are starting a business?

Surround yourself with a strong support team. So you can always think like an owner even when you have to act like an employee.

What do you like best about owning a business?

Every day I get to make a difference in someone's life. The excitement of creating a vision, implementing the vision and watching it become a reality is the best reward.

Q&A

What are your most popular products or services?
Miniature pastries for events and weddings as well as cake balls, French macaroons and special occasion cakes are some of Tart's most popular items.

What do you CRAVE?
I crave good food and family time. Some of the best memories we have are from the time spent when we're all around the table.

What motivates you on a daily basis?
My family motivates me to work hard, and I love what I do, so it makes it easy to get going in the mornings.

How do you relax?
I love to travel in order to get full relaxation and let my mind take a break.

Tart Bakery

Bluffview, Dallas

Elegant. Decadent. Sweet.

Tart offers a wide assortment of desserts that are as mouth-watering as they are aesthetically divine. They have become known for flourless chocolate truffle cakes, cake balls and Parisian-style French macaroons. For the indecisive shopper, or someone looking to appease a few different cravings at once, Tart provides a visually arresting assortment of delicious miniature pastries, including lemon meringue tartlets, éclairs and heavenly petits fours.

Specialties: French Pastries, Cakes, Cookies and Gifts
5219 W Lovers Lane, Ste B, Dallas
469.335.8919, tartbakerydallas.com

Photos by Natalie Pitts

Elizabeth Fenimore and Dorit Suffness

Q&A

What tip would you give women who are starting a business?
Keep your head up and your overhead down.

What do you like best about owning a business?
By taking responsibility and having the authority to back it up, we lay the foundation for our own success.

What is your biggest fear?
People not realizing the importance of print materials for promoting their business, institution or cause. (And being forced to use the font Comic Sans.)

What motivates you on a daily basis?
Finding great, creative ideas in unexpected places.

ThinkHaus Creative, Inc.

North Dallas

Innovative. Effective. Savvy.
ThinkHaus Creative is a service-oriented graphic design group providing smart communication for corporations, retailers, educational institutions and not-for-profits. ThinkHaus guides clients through branding, marketing, print and interactive media while being mindful of environmental impact. Their nationally award-winning team of creatives delivers something extra: diversity of thought and experience that adds up to results.

Specialty: Graphic Design
By appointment: 12655 N Central Expressway, Ste 317, Dallas
214.217.5300, thinkhauscreative.com
facebook.com/thinkhauscreative, Twitter: @thinkhauscreative
linkedin.com/company/thinkhaus-creative-inc

Portrait and upper right photo by Elle Parks Photography

Photo by Elle Parks Photography

"Our role model is anyone who manages to do great work and balance life at the same time."

—Elizabeth Fenimore and Dorit Suffness of ThinkHaus Creative, Inc.

Tsada Yoga

Downtown, Dallas

Healing. Unconventional. Inspiring.

A uniquely beautiful studio complete with creative, talented, nurturing teachers and a delightfully diverse clientele, Tsada offers an eclectic mix of fun and fundamentally strong yoga, Yogua Dao, T'ai Chi and meditation. Perhaps best known for its weekly YogaUnderground, a socially conscious and community-oriented class created to cultivate healing energies and vitality, Tsada unites us with Mother Nature and each other.

Photos by Catie Ronquillo

Q&A

What do you CRAVE?

A peaceful, happy mind because from a place of serenity and joy, challenges become adventurous and opportunities and successes are fully experienced and appreciated.

Who is your role model or mentor?

Charlie, an absolutely beautiful and amazing woman who once asked me "and what is it you want to do?" And when I explained, she said "so when do we start?"

What is your motto or theme song?

A friend once said to me, "Drop your bucket where you are." Although it sounds strange, it works for me. Envision ahead, and then start where you are.

Photos by Katie Cassidy Photography

Turner Online Design

Dallas, Texas

Smart. Streamlined. Effective.

Turner Online Design has a knack for creating top-of-the-line websites or blogs for bargain prices. Specializing in SEO-friendly websites or blogs, Facebook and Twitter business pages, small business e-mail networking and e-mail marketing campaigns, Turner Online Design can help your small business or hobby grow to the next level.

Mackenzie Turner

Q&A

What are your most popular products or services?
Websites, hosted and non-hosted blogs, Facebook and Twitter design, business e-mail networking, e-mail marketing and SEO.

What tip would you give women who are starting a business?
Stay focused and true to who you are. Really listen to the people who inspire and ground you. And have fun!

What do you like best about owning a business?
Being able to work from my laptop on the couch or outside on a beautiful day.

How do you relax?
A great massage and a glass of wine does it every time!

Specialties: Website Design, Online Marketing Presence
469.955.4173, turneronlinedesign.com
Twitter: @tonlinedesign

Twenty-Two Fifty Interiors

Sugar Land, Texas

Timeless. Detailed. Innovative.
Twenty-Two Fifty Interiors was opened by a local mother/daughter team to house their dream of creating a design studio and retail space that inspired the imagination. "Beauty is in the details," and this designing duo gives attention to each detail in every project, whether it be a home in the Houston area or a vacation home. The retail space is filled with unique accessories, furniture and gifts. The recently launched online store allows shoppers across the country access to Teena and Lauren's latest market finds, and offers free domestic ground shipping or in-store pickup.

Specialties: Design Services, Furniture, Jewelry, Accessories
2250 Lone Star Drive, Sugar Land, 281.265.2250
twentytwofiftyinteriors.com
facebook.com/TwentyTwoFiftyInteriors, Twitter: @2250interiors

Photos by Tiffany Kowalski Photography, except portrait courtesy of UpClose Magazine

Teena and Lauren Caldwell

Q&A

What are your most popular products or services?
Our design services, which are tailored to every client, and our jewelry from designers such as VSA, Chan Luu and local designers.

What is your favorite part of owning a business?
As a mother/daughter team, the most rewarding thing is to see your dreams take flight... this is truly our dreams of over 10 years, and it's finally a reality!

What is your motto or theme song?
"I'm a survivor!" People thought we were crazy for opening a new business in not the best of economic times, but we have survived, and we're expanding!

Q&A

Who is your role model or mentor?
My mom and grandmother taught me that any obstacle can be overcome. They showed me that learning should never end. They taught me to always stay humble and enthusiastic.

What is your biggest fear?
My biggest fear is not consciously knowing my fears. Once I realize they are there, I can handle them and work on overcoming them.

What tip would you give women who are starting a business?
Truly connect and know people rather than just network. It will create lifelong supporters who are more than willing to share you and your business with other people.

Uptown Mediation

McKinney, Texas

Fresh. Diverse. Motivated.

Uptown Mediation provides worldwide dispute resolution for families, businesses and communities. The headquarters is located in McKinney, Texas, with a second office in NYC. Also available worldwide and online. Owner Amanda Lipscomb put together a team of mediators who provide an unprecedented combination of peacemaking, leading the way for trends and expansion. Multilingual, day, night, weekend and online appointments are available.

Specialties: Mediation, Alternative Dispute Resolution
469.342.8825, UptownMediation.com
facebook.com/UptownMediation
Twitter: @UptownMediation
linkedin.com/in/UptownMediation

Photos by Catie Ronquillo, except portrait by Kelly Caldwell

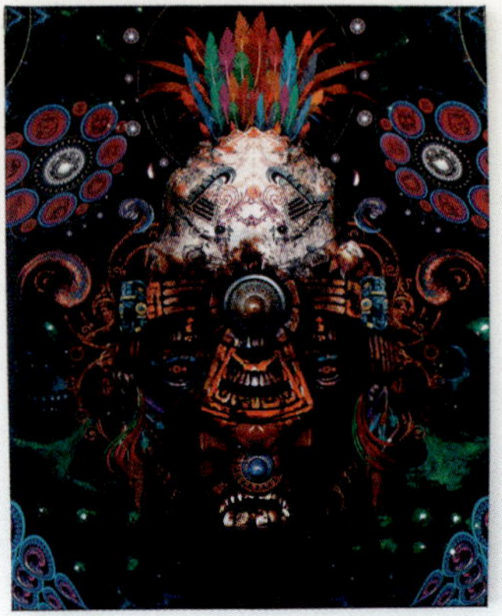

Q&A

What are your most popular products or services?
Paintings, sculptures, mixed media, illustrations, prints and commissioned pieces are the most popular, but we also rent the space for wellness groups, wine tasting and connecting with the community.

What tip would you give women who are starting a business?
Know what you are getting into. Prepare the best you can. Have interns and great people working for you who have the same passion or dream. Separate work from home.

What do you like best about owning a business?
Creating, being a visionary, bringing others' dreams to life, sharing, connecting and helping others heal through art.

WAAS Gallery

East Dallas, Dallas

Positive. Empowering. Creative.

Located in the epicenter of the recently reburgeoning Deep Ellum and Fair Park neighborhoods, WAAS Gallery is a unique and exuberant new voice within the Dallas art community. Their commitment to both the artist and a buyer-friendly platform sets WAAS apart. As a business, they are dedicated to showcasing exciting, relevant and innovative work from significant artists hailing from local and international markets.

Specialty: Fine Art
By appointment only: 2722 Logan St, Dallas
626.731.LOVE (5683)
waasgallery.com, brandyadamsmakeup.com, facebook.com/waasgallery, Twitter: @waasgallery

Photos by Natalie Pitts
Art by David Carmichel, Eva Montealegre, Jonathan Ramirez, Kevin Lewis Fougerrousse and Josh King

The {well} Summit

Dallas, Texas

Inspirational. Creative. Chic.

The {well} Summit is the vision of two entrepreneurs who have a passion to bring faith and work together. The {well} is a community of women entrepreneurs who love the Lord and desire to do work, life and love well... not perfectly but {well}. It is built through inspiration, education and resources, culminating in a fall conference that brings women together called The {well} Summit.

Kelly Rucker and Jenn Sprinkle

Q&A

What tip would you give women who are starting a business?

Kelly: Get a website and an online presence. Find beneficial networking events, and start making connections!

Jenn: Cut out the time-wasters and focus on the profit-makers.

What place inspires you?

Kelly: The mountains. I am reminded how small I am in comparison to all creation.

What do you CRAVE?

Jenn: More time, authentic friendships and inspiring others to pursue their dreams.

How do you relax?

Jenn: The spa and watching my favorite TV shows.

Kelly: Spending time with my husband and enjoying a glass of wine.

Specialties: Community, Consulting, Education, Resources
thewellsummit.com, facebook.com/theWELLSummit
Twitter: @TheWellSummit

Specialties: Baby and Children's Clothing, Gifts, Photography
2014 S Goliad, Ste 138, Rockwall, 972.722.5911
wonderfullymadechildrens.com
facebook.com/wonderfullymadechildrens

Photos by Natalie Pitts

Wonderfully Made
Children's Boutique & Photo Studio

Rockwall, Texas

Fun. Original. Devoted.
Wonderfully Made Children's Boutique & Photo Studio features a unique experience. It's a vintage-styled boutique with a modern portrait studio where the owner, Alison, hosts custom-tailored sessions for newborns, children and families. From the most unique or essential children's fashions (sizes Preemie–14) and accessories to the newest baby product or diaper bag for Mom- or Dad-to-Be, Wonderfully Made definitely has something for everyone!

Q&A

What tip would you give women who are starting a business?
Ask yourself, "What would you attempt to do if you knew you could not fail?"

What motivates you on a daily basis?
The satisfaction that my customers get from an awesome experience in the store. I come in contact with many situations, and it's motivating to reflect on how I tackled each one.

What are your most popular products or services?
The NoseFrida and Padilily move out the door by the dozen—each a great gender-neutral gift. We are the baby and shower gift destination east of Dallas!

Young Wealth Management

Dallas, Texas

Skilled. Practical. Professional.
Young Wealth Management's commitment to professionalism and the cooperative development of unique, personal goals forms the foundation of any strong financial plan. A cornerstone of financial planning is the recognition that everyone's economic and life situation is unique. Personalized service is essential when matching clients with the right financial products and services. Securities and advisory services offered through LPL Financial, a registered investment advisor, member FINRA/SIPC.

Specialty: Wealth Management
214.785.2317, lpl.com/linda.young
linda.young@lpl.com
linkedin.com/in/youngwealthmanagement

Photos by Katie Cassidy Photography

Q&A

What are your most popular products or services?
Individual financial, tax and retirement planning; evaluating investment and insurance products, asset allocation and client portfolio management; strategies planning for business continuity; transfer estate planning, wealth transfer and executive compensation planning.

What motivates you on a daily basis?
Creating a financial plan that reflects the owner's stage of life, whether purchasing a first home, financing a child's college education or planning for retirement.

Index by Category

The Arts

Beauty

Business Services

by Category (continued)

by Category (continued)

Index by Neighborhood

by Neighborhood (continued)

by Neighborhood (continued)

Contributors

We believe in acknowledging, celebrating and passionately supporting locally owned businesses and entrepreneurs. We are grateful to all contributors for this publication.

Melody Biringer

CRAVE Founder

thecravecompany.com, startupjunkie.com

Innovative. Feminine. Connective.

Melody Biringer, self-avowed "start-up junkie," has built companies that range from Biringer Farm, a family-run specialty-food business, to home furnishings to a fitness studio.

Her current entrepreneurial love-child is The CRAVE Company: designed to creatively connect entrepreneurs who approach business in a fresh new way with the consumers they desire, as well as with each other. CRAVE is a resource for women entrepreneurs to promote their business and support like-minded women, and CRAVEguides are your go-to source for anything you could ever wish to find in your city—exclusively from women. Melody has taken CRAVE from Seattle to more than 20 cities worldwide, including New York City, Boston, Los Angeles, Chicago, Amsterdam and Toronto. Melody is a loyal community supporter, versed traveler and strong advocate for women-owned businesses.

Jenn Sprinkle

CRAVE Dallas Partner

jennsprinkle.com, Twitter: @jenn_sprinkle

Passionate. Creative. Ambitious.

Jenn was born a serial entrepreneur: when playing store and office as a child, Jenn even made her own receipt books with perforated pages. She has been a longtime supporter and champion of entrepreneurs and loves encouraging business owners with their dreams. Jenn was so impressed by the women she met through the first edition of CRAVE Dallas that she took on the challenge of curating the second edition. Once again, she has been blessed beyond belief by knowing many of the women she has met through this community. Some of these women have become her dearest and closest friends to this day; she will be eternally grateful for these relationships.

Alison Turner, *Graphic Designer*

alisonjturner.com, linkedin.com/in/alisont

Alison is a passionate designer and critical thinker from Seattle. She supports human rights and the local food movement. She enjoys researching interesting things, volunteering, being outside, dancing, cooking and running.

Amanda Buzard, *Lead Designer*

amandabuzard.com, linkedin.com/in/amandabuzard

Amanda is a Seattle native with a thirst for learning, tinkering and experimenting. She chases many creative and active pursuits in her spare time, including photography, baking, attempting DIY projects and exploring her favorite cities: Seattle and San Francisco.

Carrie Wicks, *Copy Editor*

linkedin.com/in/carriewicks

Carrie has been proofreading professionally for 14-plus years in mostly creative fields. When she's not proofreading/copyediting, she's reading, singing jazz, walking in the woods or gardening.

Catie Ronquillo, *Photographer*

catieronquillo.com, catieronquillo.com/blog, Twitter: @catieronquillo

Catie loves red velvet cupcakes, Disney movies, hanging out with her husband and spoiling her dog. She believes that all people and relationships should be celebrated in a way that reflects their brilliance; she strives to pinpoint what makes you unique through beautiful, lasting images.

Elle Parks, *Photographer*

elleparksphotography.com, Twitter: @elleparksphoto

Elle has a deep-rooted passion for photography, fashion, people and storytelling. She has been privileged with hands-on experience in New York City, Italy, France and Dallas: merging worlds together to tell a dreamy story.

Katie Cassidy Photography, *Photographer*

214.585.2448, kcassidyphotography.com
facebook.com/kcassidyphotography

Katie is a wedding photographer serving the Dallas area with full wedding coverage. Katie combines artistic talent and love for storytelling to capture your day that's overflowing with love, beauty and emotion.

Kelly Rucker Photography, *Photographer*

kellyrucker.com, kelly@kellyrucker.com, Twitter: @kelrucker

Kelly's passion for photography was inspired at a young age, by her father. The simple gift of a camera birthed in her a love for art, entrepreneurship and people.

Matt & Julie Weddings, *Photographer*

mattandjulieweddings.com, Twitter: @mattjulienorine
Instagram: @julienorine

Julie is a wedding photographer who joyfully works alongside her husband, Matt. When Julie isn't photographing people in love, she enjoys traveling, cooking, drinking coffee on a patio and snuggling with her cat, Pucci.

Natalie Pitts Photography, *Photographer*

972.342.9529, nataliepittsphotography.com, natalie3r@gmail.com,

Natalie is a professional photographer in the Dallas area specializing in portrait and wedding photography. She captures the true personalities of her subjects and provides quality images that her clients can enjoy for a lifetime.

Special thanks to Claire McCormack Photography and Morgan Jordan Photography.

CRAVE DALLAS

Get the savings you crave with the following participating businesses—one time only!

- [ ] 2shea Boutique
20% discount
- [ ] A Well Dressed Home
$50 off an online design board
- [ ] Ashley Russell & Company Salon
20% off all services
- [ ] Asian Mint
Free order of dumplings with a purchase of two entrees
- [ ] Biosanes Nutrition and Health
20% off your first order. Call 1-888-670-5433 to redeem
- [ ] Bookkeeper Girl
$25 coupon towards conversion fee
- [ ] Boundless Collection
10% off your first order
- [ ] Cassie's Frozen Yogurt
10% discount on catering
- [ ] Chalkboard China
20% off your online purchase
- [ ] Coco Fleur Events
10% discount
- [ ] Cole London
50% off Cole London stationery
- [ ] ComputerTutor4Seniors.com
Buy one month of "Keep Us On Call" and get one month free
- [ ] Creative Oasis Coaching
Free session with purchase of coaching package
- [ ] Cuptastic!
15% discount
- [ ] Custom Laser Engravers, LLC
20% discount
- [ ] Dancing Angels Studio
One free class
- [ ] Deanie Michelle Events
20% discount
- [ ] Ditto Boutique
25% discount
- [ ] Ebony Peoples Events & Design
10% discount
- [ ] Elle Parks
15% off creative commercial package
- [ ] Ellis Art Gallery
20% discount
- [ ] Facelogic Spa
20% discount
- [ ] Fairy Godmother Bridal Agency
20% discount
- [ ] Fashion Fix Style
20% off your first Fashion Fix
- [ ] The Festive Kitchen
10% discount in-store
- [ ] Fihankra Dance & Fitness Studio
25% discount
- [ ] Frosted Pink Cake Company
10% discount
- [ ] Get Noticed Boutique
20% discount
- [ ] High Maintenance "Couture in a Can"
15% off hostess discount for "Can Party"
- [ ] Hitched Events
10% off any wedding planning package
- [ ] Humanistic Consulting
Complimentary HR audit
- [ ] Inwood Chiropractic Center
50% off first visit
- [ ] Jenn Sprinkle Creative
10% discount
- [ ] Jordan Filloon
20% discount
- [ ] Julep
20% off one regularly priced item

- [ ] Katie Cassidy Photography
  Free bridal session with booked wedding package
- [ ] Kelly Rucker Photography
  10% off portrait session
- [ ] Kim Rozell Makeup Design
  $25 discount on services
- [ ] La Bella Belly Pregnancy Spa & Ultrasound Center
  15% discount (up to $20) on any one service
- [ ] Living Well Health & Wellness Center
  20% off a 3-month trial of a Be Well membership
- [ ] Lotus Soap
  15% discount
- [ ] Megan Adams
  15% discount (excluding works of art)
- [ ] Movida Boutique
  15% discount
- [ ] Naila Malik, MD
  10% off any one regularly priced service or product
- [ ] Nan Lee Jewelry
  Free shipping on online orders
- [ ] Natalie Pitts Photography
  $30 off a photo session
- [ ] Nine-Eighteen
  20% off all fashion jewelry
- [ ] Occhiali Modern Optics
  15% discount
- [ ] Park Cities Dance
  $20 discount on any class (first-time clients only)
- [ ] Pieces
  20% off one item
- [ ] Pilates Connection
  15% off purchase of a session or class package
- [ ] PLAN B PR
  25% off your first class
- [ ] Prewitt Family Dentistry
  Free bleaching trays at new patient exam
- [ ] Primp Salon*Boutique*Garden
  $10 discount
- [ ] Random
  20% discount
- [ ] Say it with Sugar Cake Shop
  10% discount
- [ ] She Reigns
  15% discount
- [ ] Shop Ten 25
  20% discount
- [ ] SitterCentralDallas
  20% discount
- [ ] The Spa Bar
  $75 off a 4-hour event
- [ ] Storyopolis Entertainment
  10% discount on art prints
- [ ] The Style House
  25% off any one item
- [ ] Styled & Organized Living
  1 free hour of professional organizing services
- [ ] Susan Posnick Cosmetics
  20% discount online
- [ ] Sweet Bee Candy Emporium
  15% discount
- [ ] Sweet Firefly Gourmet Ice Cream and Candied Treats
  20% discount
- [ ] TrueBeautyRx
  20% discount
- [ ] Tsada Yoga
  50% off one all-access monthly membership
- [ ] Turner Online Design
  $200 off any website or blog design
- [ ] Twenty-Two Fifty Interiors
  15% discount
- [ ] Wonderfully Made Children's Boutique & Photo Studio
  Free gift with purchase

Use code CRAVE for online discount when applicable.

Details of discounts may vary from business to business, so please call first. The CRAVE company shall not be held responsible for variations on discounts at individual businesses. This page may not be photocopied or otherwise duplicated.